Dubai

Front cover: Emirates Towers

Right: The ancient skill of falconry is still popular

TOP 10 ATTRACTIONS

Burj Al Arab • The 'seven-star' hotel is the city's architectural icon *(page 68)*

Nad Al Sheba • The venue for the world's richest horse race, the Dubai World Cup *(page 74)*, held in March each year

4x4 adventures • A great way to explore the desert interior *(page 83)*

Sheikh Zayed Road • Its futuristic skyline is home to some of the world's tallest buildings *(page 54)*

Bastakiya • Traditional wind-tower houses are the attraction in the city's restored historic quarter *(page 34)*

The Gold Souk • Pick up a glittering souvenir of Dubai in this world-famous shopping quarter *(page 40)*

Jumeira Strip • Trendy boutiques and cafés line this popular area *(page 63)*

Abras (water taxis) • Enjoy an *abra* ride between the traditional souks on either side of Dubai Creek *(page 37)*

Hatta Heritage Village • Just an hour away from the city *(page 78)*

Madinat Jumeirah • A fabulous re-creation of old Arabia, with souks, galleries, restaurants, cafés and canals *(page 70)*

CONTENTS

94

54

100

Features

62

32

96

INTRODUCTION

From the back-lot trailers of Hollywood to the changing rooms of British football's Premiership, a once unfamiliar name has entered the lexicon of the world's rich and famous – Dubai. If you can't find the city on a map, open a newspaper or glossy magazine and the chances are you'll find it there. Dubai will be in the story about the famous footballer who has bought a house on a property development that's visible from space, or the two Hollywood stars who fuelled rumours of a romance by checking into the world's tallest hotel together.

Few people had heard of Dubai in the last decade of the 20th century. Then, if anyone knew anything at all, it was that the emirate had oil and an airport with luxury cars in the duty-free shop. Today, however, this rapidly expanding, cleverly marketed hub for business and tourism in the Middle East has become a global destination of choice for the likes of the Beckhams, and Brad and Angelina. Bayern Munich and Chelsea come here to train – any excuse will do.

In Dubai, you can watch Tiger Woods play golf, Roger Federer play tennis and Frankie Dettori ride home the winners within days of each other. You might even squeeze in a gig by a rock legend or contemporary chart topper. Dubai has its own international film festival and hosts the headquarters of world cricket, which moved here in 2005 after 96 years in the hallowed home of the sport, Lord's in London.

For a city that was little known when many of its longer-term expatriates began their contracts here, it all seems so, well, unlikely. But that's Dubai. The ambitious, alluring starlet of world tourism has worked for decades to become the

Fishermen on Deira quayside

overnight success that everyone's now hearing about, enhancing her skyline and her coastline to become more attractive to the jet-set, package-holiday visitors and business travellers. A former hardship posting, Dubai is becoming the Monaco of the Middle East. You never know who you might see in the next car at traffic lights, or bump into in a lift at the latest luxury hotel. The white-haired man at Arrivals who looks like Bill Clinton probably is Bill Clinton.

On the Map

If you turn to a map instead of the gossip column, property section or the sports pages of your daily newspaper, you'll find Dubai on the northern shore of the Arabian peninsula at around 25°N 55°E. It's sometimes shown as 'Dibai' or 'Dubayy' on maps, a spelling that's closer to how the locals pronounce it.

Palm Jumeirah, one of Dubai's extraordinary Palm Islands

Dubai is capital of the second largest of the seven emirates, or sheikhdoms, that comprise the United Arab Emirates (UAE). Located northeast of the federal capital, Abu Dhabi, on the southern shores of the Arabian Gulf, Dubai faces Iran and has an eastern land border with Oman. The emirate covers 3,885 sq km (1,500 sq miles) of flat coastal plain and rolling desert dunes, with barren mountains, the Hajar range, in the distant east, around the Dubai enclave of Hatta.

At 72km (45 miles), Dubai's natural coastline is relatively short. The Jumeira district, in the south of the city, has fine, sandy beaches packed with the luxury resort hotels that have helped establish Dubai as the Middle East's second most popular tourism destination (after Egypt). Further along the coast at Jebel Ali, the biggest man-made port in the world – capable of handling seven million containers from 125 shipping lines in 71 berths – has helped maintain the city's historic credentials as a strategically located centre for trade.

With space for new crowd-pulling resorts rapidly running out, the coastline is being dramatically extended by the creation of three artificial palm-shaped islands, a man-made archipelago shaped like a map of the world, and a new waterfront district bordering Abu Dhabi. These mind-boggling land-reclamation projects, undertaken by local property developer Nakheel at the instigation of Sheikh Mohammed Bin Rashid Al Maktoum, who succeeded his brother as ruler of the emirate in 2006, have but one aim: to enlarge the playground for the 15 million annual visitors expected in Dubai by 2010.

Sunshine and Shopping

Dubai's central location and expanding tourism infrastructure are not the only things luring visitors from northern and southern hemispheres. A year-round holiday destination has to offer great weather – Dubai is blessed with 12 months of sunshine. It's true that in summer, from June to September, the mercury

Dubai girls in Creekside Park

can hit 48°C (118°F), with high humidity on the coast, limiting the time anyone can spend outdoors. But from October to May, Dubai's arid, sub-tropical climate is very pleasant, with maximum daytime temperatures ranging from 24° to 37°C (75–99°F), with low humidity and limited rainfall.

Another major draw is shopping – Dubai is the proverbial shoppers' paradise. All the world's major brands are represented in an ever-increasing number of stylish malls across the city. Mall of the Emirates on Sheikh Zayed Road, Ibn Battuta Mall in Jebel Ali, the BurJuman extension in Bur Dubai, the Italian-themed Mercato Mall in Jumeira and the atmospheric Souk Madinat Jumeirah on the coast are more recent additions to old favourites Deira City Centre, Wafi Mall and the chic Emirates Towers Boulevard. At 836,000 sq m (9m sq ft), The Dubai Mall in the Burj Dubai development on Sheikh Zayed Road is currently enjoying the title of 'world's largest mall'; though the Mall of Arabia in Dubailand will also vie for the top spot.

Booming Business

Historically, Dubai was a city of merchants even before oil was discovered in the emirate in 1966. As long ago as 1894, Sheikh Maktoum Bin Hasher Al Maktoum used low customs duties to entice merchants from Iran, Baluchistan in present-day Pakistan and India to settle in the city. In the early years of the 20th century, Dubai grew prosperous on trade, particularly in pearls and gold. But the massive wealth that many associate with the modern Gulf only came to Dubai after 1969, when oil production began. Oil production peaked at 410,000 barrels per day in 1991, and has been in decline ever since. In fact, experts predict that Dubai's oil reserves will run out by 2010.

This city was built on oil, but facing a future without income from 'black gold', the ruling Maktoum family ordered a strategic shift in Dubai's economy away from its decades-old dependence on hydrocarbons to business, commerce and tourism. Key to this strategy has been the creation of business free-zones, such as Dubai International Financial Centre (DIFC), Dubai Internet City, Dubai Media City, Knowledge Village and Dubai Studio City. Major global players have relocated their regional offices to Dubai, pushing the number of nationalities resident in the city to almost 200 and the overall population to between one and two million (up from 689,420 in 1995), of which expatriates outnumber Emiratis by more than eight to one. This restructuring of the economy has been so successful that by 2008, the non-oil sector contributed 96 percent of Gross Domestic Product (GDP).

Heat Couture

UAE national dress is worn in the workplace, at home and when out and about. The men's white, floor-length robe is known as the *kandoora* or *dishdash*. The cloth headdress, which can be white or red-and-white check, is a *gutra* secured by a stiff black cord known as an *agal*, with which their *bedu* ancestors hobbled their camels' legs. Increasingly among young men baseball caps are replacing the *gutra* and *agal*. The most visible items of women's clothing are the floor-length black cloak, the *abaya*, and headscarf, called a *sheyla*. Older women may be seen wearing the stiff gold and lacquer face mask known as a *burqa*, though this is increasingly rare. Children often dress in Western-style clothes.

Modern Dubai is a vibrant destination for leisure or business, one of a number of new 'city brands' that is compared favourably to Singapore, which it has emulated in so many ways, from shopping festivals to land reclamation. Admittedly, it is undergoing some growing pains, traffic congestion among them – what was once a 15-minute cross-town car journey can now take more than an hour – but planned improvements in public transport, including an elevated Dubai Metro light railway, will accompany the ambitious projects that are being realised before visitors' eyes. One such project is the world's tallest building, Burj Dubai, which on completion is expected to be 818m (2,684ft) high.

The desert is never far away

Notable possibilities for day trips from the city include the Dubai Desert Conservation Reserve, with its herds of protected oryx, and the oasis of Hatta, an hour's drive inland. The neighbouring emirate of Sharjah, with its Blue Souk, heritage quarter, art galleries and aircraft museum is less than an hour's drive along the coast, while the less prosperous emirates of Ajman, Umm Al Qaiwain and Ras Al Khaimah, further north, provide a glimpse of what life in Dubai must have been like long before its name entered the lexicon of the rich and famous.

A BRIEF HISTORY

The character of modern Dubai is rooted in its history, and its history is trade. At the outset of the 21st century, it is tempting to view the ruling Maktoum family's headline-grabbing initiatives to develop and promote the city in the context of the massive oil wealth accrued since 1969 and the urgent need to prepare for a future without oil, as the emirate's reserves run dry.

But the current economic strategy of using free-zone incentives to attract foreign investment is exactly what previous generations of Maktoums were doing long before oil was discovered. In fact, what we now call Dubai was an international centre for the re-export of luxury goods pre-motor car, pre-oil, pre-Maktoum and even pre-Islam.

It would be quite wrong to underplay the enormous impact that oil has had on society – in the second half of the 20th century oil wealth financed massive public-works projects and facilitated Dubai's emergence as a major world city – but to regard modern Dubai at the tail-end of its oil era as being very different in character from the city of the 1890s, just because it's bigger now and better known, is to misunderstand what really fuels it: not oil, but the realisation that there's money to be made in welcoming foreigners.

One theory holds that the name 'Dubai' is derived from a word for money, though it may originate in the Farsi for 'two brothers', namely the two districts on either side of

Oil wealth

Dubai's oil was formed during the Cretaceous period, around 144–66 million years ago. It gave Dubai its great wealth during the second half of the 20th century, but by 2008, oil accounted for only 4 percent of Dubai's Gross Domestic Product (GDP).

Sassanid and Abbasid-era ruins, at Jumeira archaeological site

the seawater creek that has been the traditional centre of trade for the past two centuries – Bur Dubai and Deira.

Foreign Influence

The location of what is now the United Arab Emirates (UAE) on the trade routes between the ancient civilisations of southern Mesopotamia (present-day Iraq) and the Indus Valley, and later between Europe and the Eastern colonies, ensured that the region has welcomed, traded with and been influenced by foreign visitors for several millennia.

Throughout history, the area that today comprises the UAE and northern Oman was known by various names. To the Sumerians of southern Mesopotamia it was Magan, famous for its copper in the 3rd millennium BC. To the Persians of the 1st millennium BC, ruled by the Biblical king Darius the Great (521–486BC), Magan was Maka, which they incorporated into their empire in the 6th century BC.

Soldiers from Magan fought alongside Darius's successor, his son Xerxes, in the battle of Doriscus in 480BC.

To the 5th-century Greek historian Herodotus the region was Mykoi. A century or so later, the sailors of Alexander the Great's navy, which explored the coast on their return from the Indus Valley, nicknamed the inhabitants *Ichthyophagi*, or 'Fish-Eaters'. The Roman-era Greek historian and geographer Strabo of Amaseia (*c*.64BC–AD21) referred to the coast as the 'promontory of the Macae in Arabia'.

To the Persian Sassanids, or Sassanians, of the 3rd to the 7th century AD it was Mazun, the 27th land of their empire. From the 4th century AD to the Islamic conquest of the 7th century, a significant number of its Sassanid-era inhabitants were Christians. The early church knew the UAE coast as Bet Mazunaye, and established monasteries along it. One of these, on Sir Bani Yas island in the emirate of Abu Dhabi, has been excavated and preserved.

In the late Sassanid era, a pre-Islamic trading post, a stop on the trade route between Mesopotamia and Oman, was established in what is now the Jumeira district of Dubai. Excavations at an 8-hectare (20-acre) site inland from the present-day Beach Park have revealed the foundations of a Sassanid governor's palace, houses built of beach rock *(farush)* and covered with lime plaster, and a marketplace. The settlement was subsequently expanded by the Abbasids in the early Islamic era. As a hub for East-West trade, under first the Sassanids then the Abbasids, Jumeira would have seen luxuries such as copper, spices, frankincense, sandalwood and teak move west, probably by sea, and valuable cargoes of gold, silver and textiles heading in the other direction.

To 18th-century European explorers, the UAE was the Coast of Julfar, named after the prominent port of the day, the birthplace of the legendary Arab navigator Ahmad Ibn Majid, near present-day Ras Al Khaimah.

In the 19th century, attacks on British cargo ships by the sea-faring Qawasim tribe of the northern emirates prompted Britain to call the region the Pirate Coast. Then, after truces were signed with local sheikhs from 1820, it became the Trucial Coast. Before the formation of the UAE in 1971, its seven sheikhdoms were known as Trucial Oman.

Early Civilisation

Though there are three important archaeological sites within Dubai's city limits – at Al Qusais near the airport, on the Jumeira coast and at Al Sufouh, further south towards Dubai Marina – much of what we know about the region's early history comes from finds at other UAE sites since the late 1950s.

The earliest evidence of human habitation is a dwelling in Dalma, Abu Dhabi, dating back 6,000 years. Subsequent discoveries of prehistoric painted pottery pieces in the northern emirates of Sharjah, Umm Al Qaiwain and Ras Al Khaimah suggest that some form of international trade existed between the inhabitants of the coastal villages and the pre-Sumerian Ubaid civilisation, which flourished in southern Mesopotamia from 5600 to 3900BC. Archaeological finds in Dalma reveal that fishing was a way of life on the coast, so it is possible that local dried fish was bartered for the Ubaid pottery or its contents. Meanwhile, on the other side of Dubai, in Umm Al Qaiwain, archaeological evidence suggests a pearl trade existed in the 5th millennium BC.

Away from the coast, between the 5th and 3rd millennia BC the inhabitants of the interior appear to have been herders who also hunted wild game. The bones of domesticated sheep, goats and cattle as well as flint arrowheads and knives have been found, especially at sites around the oasis city of Al Ain. These suggest a people who were hunter-gatherers, supplementing what their herds provided – meat, milk, hair, fleece and leather – with game such as gazelle, oryx and wild camel.

Umm Al Nar Period

One of the most famous arch-aeological sites in the UAE is Umm Al Nar (meaning 'Mother of Fire'), near Abu Dhabi, a third-millennium BC Bronze Age settlement that has given its name to the period in UAE history between 2700 and 2000BC. Camel bones found here and dated to 2500–2200BC are thought to be the earliest evidence in the world for the domestication of the camel, a revolutionary development in overland transportation that would not be surpassed for 4,000 years, until the first four-wheel-drive vehicles were introduced in the late 1940s and '50s.

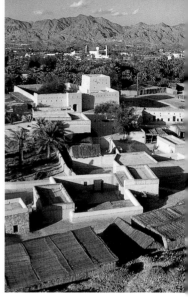

Hatta Heritage Village dates back 3,000 years

A significant Umm Al Nar-era site in Dubai is at Al Sufouh, between Jumeira and the towering high rises of Dubai Marina. In the early 1990s, a circular Umm Al Nar-type tomb and settlement was excavated here by an Australian team working with Dubai Municipality. Other sites from the Umm Al Nar period include Mowaihat, in Ajman emirate, and Tell Abraq, on the border of Sharjah and Umm Al Qaiwain. Artefacts found at Tell Abraq since 1989 – from the Indus Valley, Mesopotamia, Iran and Afghanistan, and including Barbar pottery typical of Dilmun (present-day Bahrain) – provide evidence of the coast's contact with the outside world.

Iron Men

During the Iron Age, between 1200 and 300BC, the population of the Emirates would have been the largest up to that point in its history. Numerous mud-brick villages of the period, unearthed by archaeologists in the second half of the 20th century, include Al Qusais in Dubai, which is probably the site of a Bronze Age community resettled. Sites further inland point to a large, agriculturally based population that cultivated cereals, raised sheep, goats and cattle, and tapped the underground freshwater supplies of the Hajar Mountains by means of the *falaj* system of irrigation channels.

During the Hellenistic era, from around 300BC to a century or so after the time of Christ, two of the most important cities were Mleiha, south of Dhaid in Sharjah emirate, which was first excavated in 1973, and Ad-Dour, near Umm Al Qaiwain, which is the largest pre-Islamic site on the Gulf coast and a candidate for the great city of Omana, mentioned by Strabo and Pliny The Elder (*c*.AD23–79). Finds at these locations include Greek pottery, wine-jar handles from Rhodes, and Roman glass. Aramaic lettering on much of the coinage found at Mleiha and Ad-Dour, as well as on stone and bronze inscriptions, indicates that the language of Christ was the lingua franca of the region in the pre-Islamic era, spread initially by dominant empires such as the Sassanids, and becoming the principal liturgical language after the Christianisation of the Bet Mazunaye region.

Ibn, Bin and Bint

In Arabic names, 'Bin' and 'Ibn' both mean 'son of': Mohammed Bin Rashid is Mohammed son of Rashid. 'Bint' is 'daughter of'.

The Islamic Era

Arabic replaced Aramaic after the region converted to Islam in AD632. The first of the Muslim Arab dynasties was the Umayyad Caliphate, which ruled in Damascus

The UAE's oldest mosque is at Badiyah on the east coast

from 661. In 749, the rival Abbasids seized power and began to exert their influence in the area, as evidenced by the early Islamic-era additions to the trading post in Jumeira, the architecture of which reflects the Abbasid style.

By the 16th century, the Persian Safavid dynasty was the dominant regional power. Coinage found in Ras Al Khaimah and Fujairah reveals that there was trade between the communities on either side of the Gulf at this time.

In the late Islamic era, thanks to the skills of Arabic navigators such as Ibn Majid, inhabitants of the region traded with East Africa, and as far as India and China, as revealed by discoveries of fine Chinese porcelain fragments at coastal sites.

European Powers

The first Europeans to impose their will in the Gulf were the Portuguese, who arrived in Oman in 1498, spread to Julfar by 1515 and remained in the region until 1633. In their 1519

Life on Dubai's creek before bridges transformed the area

map of Arabia and India, Portuguese cartographers Pedro
Reinel and Lopo Homen recorded a number of place names
that can be identified on the UAE coast today, including Mil-
licoe (Umm Al Qaiwain). The settlement they refer to as
'Oabey' may be an early reference to Dubai. The earliest certain reference to 'Dibei' was made in 1580 by the Venetian
court jeweller Gasparo Balbi, who was drawn to the region
by the quality of its pearls.

The Portuguese were followed by the Dutch, whose spice-
laden ships passed through the Gulf en route from their ter-
ritories in the Far East. In the 19th century, the British asserted
their control of the trade route to colonial India through a
series of treaties with local rulers from 1820, the most important of which were the 1853 Perpetual Treaty of Maritime
Truce, ending conflict between warring tribes and allowing
the pearl trade to flourish, and the 1892 Exclusive Agreement,
the terms of which – that Britain alone would represent the

sheikhdoms in foreign relations while guaranteeing their security and internal autonomy – remained in force until the UAE was established as an independent federation in 1971.

An early ally of the British in Dubai was Mohammed Bin Hazza, who ruled the small fishing and pearling village from his creekside Shindagha home at the time of the 1820 agreement. A British understanding with Hazza led to the first recognition on paper that Dubai was an entity separate from the more powerful communities of Abu Dhabi and Sharjah.

Enter the Maktoums

It was under the Maktoum family, who assumed power from Hazza after they broke away from Abu Dhabi in 1833, that the three settlements around the creek – Shindagha, Bur Dubai and Deira – were to prosper and grow. By the 1870s,

A Dynamic Dynasty

Dubai's phenomenal growth from the late 1950s to the present day is due to two men: Sheikh Rashid Bin Saeed Al Maktoum and his son Sheikh Mohammed. Sheikh Rashid, 'the Father of Dubai', ruled from 1958 to 1990. Even before oil was discovered, he took out loans to build an infrastructure to ensure the city was well positioned to exploit oil wealth when it came. His philosophy was: 'What is good for business is good for Dubai.' He was often seen around the city inspecting construction work on Port Rashid, Jebel Ali Port and the Dubai World Trade Centre. When he died in 1990, his eldest son Sheikh Maktoum became ruler, but it was Sheikh Mohammed, the Crown Prince, who was the new driving force behind the city's development. Regarding himself as 'the CEO of Dubai Inc', Sheikh Mohammed led the drive towards a more diversified economy. His brother died in 2006, and now 'Sheikh Mo' rules the emirate. He can often be seen driving around in his favourite white Mercedes 4x4 with the number plate '1'.

the British came to regard Dubai, rather than Sharjah, as the principal port of the Trucial States. In 1894, displaying the eye for an opportunity that has been a trait of the ruling Maktoums ever since, Sheikh Maktoum Bin Hasher Al Maktoum offered tax concessions to lure merchants from Iran, Baluchistan, in present-day Pakistan, and India. In 1902, when the authorities in Lingah, Persia, increased their customs duties, he established Dubai as a free-trade port. The influx of foreign traders gathered pace, the population grew, the people prospered and the city expanded, with revolutionary new architecture, introduced from abroad, transforming the skyline with wind-towers.

This pattern of inward investment, expansion and construction will be familiar to visitors to politically stable Dubai 100 years on – post-pearl industry and post-oil. Today, Maktoum Bin Hasher's descendants are luring foreign experts in the knowledge industries of IT, the media and financial services to 21st-century free zones such as Dubai Internet City (billed at its launch as a 'virtual creek'), Dubai Media City and Dubai International Financial Centre.

Sheikh Zayed and Sheikh Maktoum on a high-rise block

History reveals a thriving network of Gulf communities dating back some 4,000 years, spread over a wide area, and in touch with the outside world, on and off. It does much to counter a common misperception in the West, reinforced by black and white photographs of a sleepy-looking, mid-20th-century Dubai, that the region was a barren backwater before the discovery of oil.

Historical Landmarks

2700–2000BC A Bronze Age settlement is established at Al Sufouh.

1st century BC An Iron Age village is established at Al Ghusais.

6th century AD The Sassanids set up a trading post in Jumeira.

AD632 The region converts to Islam. Arabic replaces Aramaic.

1580 Earliest surviving reference to 'Dibei' by Gasparo Balbi of Venice.

1793 A dependency of Abu Dhabi, Dubai is a fishing and pearling village of 1,200 people located around the creek.

1833 Maktoum Bin Buti Al Maktoum and 800 members of the Al Bu Falasah section of the Bani Yas tribe settle in Shindagha, establishing the ruling Maktoum dynasty.

1853 The Perpetual Treaty of Maritime Truce is signed by Britain and local sheikhs. The region becomes the Trucial Coast.

1894 Sheikh Maktoum Bin Hasher encourages foreign merchants to settle in Dubai.

1902 Increased customs duties in the Persian port of Lingah prompt more foreign traders to migrate to Dubai's free-trade zone.

1912 Sheikh Saeed Bin Maktoum becomes ruler.

1950s Electricity (1952) and a police force (1956) introduced.

1958 Sheikh Rashid Bin Saeed, 'the Father of Dubai', becomes ruler.

1966 Oil is discovered in Dubai's offshore Fatah field.

1969 Oil production begins.

1971 The UAE becomes an independent federation on 2 December. Abu Dhabi's Sheikh Zayed Bin Sultan Al Nahyan is President, Sheikh Rashid Vice-President and his son, Sheikh Maktoum, Prime Minister.

1980s First mall (Al Ghurair Centre, 1981), Dubai Duty Free (1983), Emirates airline (1985) and Jebel Ali Free Zone (1985) established.

1990 Sheikh Maktoum Bin Rashid becomes ruler.

2005 Population of Dubai reaches 1.5 million, up from 59,000 in 1967.

2006 Sheikh Maktoum dies. Sheikh Mohammed becomes ruler of Dubai, and Vice-President and Prime Minister of the UAE.

2007 Burj Dubai becomes the world's tallest building on 21 July, passing the 509m (1,670ft) record set by Taipei 101.

WHERE TO GO

Dubai – pronounced 'do buy', not 'dew buy' – is an extraordinary and surprising city. The cosmopolitan home to the vast majority of the emirate's 1.5 million (and growing) population, its climate and beaches have met the two traditional holiday requirements of sun and sand for decades. Indeed, aside from the Arabian souks on Dubai Creek, at one time sun and sand were about all the city could offer.

But the government's drive to uncover, preserve or rebuild heritage sites, which was initiated in the mid-1980s and gathered pace in the '90s; the development of a fascinating skyline with camera-pleasing landmarks such as Emirates Towers and the sail-shaped Burj Al Arab hotel; the proliferation of world-class shopping malls; and the promotion of the emirate's desert interior as a 'safari' destination for rough and ready exploration or luxury, reserve-based retreats means there are now so many places of interest that visitors can find themselves with little time for the beach – though world-class resorts such as Madinat Jumeirah and One&Only Royal Mirage will surely lure them back to the turquoise waters of the Gulf eventually.

Best in show

Dubai was voted world leader in eight categories at the 2008 World Travel Awards: best destination; best cruise port; best hotel and best all-suite hotel (Burj Al Arab); best serviced apartment hotel (Grosvenor House); best spa resort (Le Royal Meridien Beach Resort & Spa); best tourism development project (Palm Jumeirah); and best suite (The Monarch). Neighbouring emirate Abu Dhabi was declared winner in two categories.

The triangular Emirates Towers loom over Dubai's skyline

Within the lifetime of its oldest residents, Dubai has grown from three settlements of palm-frond, mud-brick and coral-stone dwellings around the mouth of its 15-km (9-mile) long creek – Shindagha, Bur Dubai and Deira, little changed from the century before – to a modern metropolis that incorporates the once-distant fishing village of Jumeira, fast gaining a worldwide reputation as a playground for the rich and famous, and sprawls as far west as Jebel Ali Port, some 30km (19 miles) along the coast.

In the 1990s, the growth corridor was along Sheikh Zayed Road, south-west of the creek. Today, this eight-lane highway to Abu Dhabi boasts a number of eye-catching skyscrapers, including the tallest building in the world – Burj Dubai.

More recently, Dubai has been expanding into the sea and the desert. The Palm island projects – south-west of the city centre, off the Jumeira and Jebel Ali coasts, and a third island the

Shindagha waterfront on the western bank of the creek

size of Manhattan on the Deira coast, just north of the creek – will add more residential neighbourhoods and resorts to the city. An area known as 'New Dubai' is fast developing inland from Jebel Ali along Emirates Road, with gated, themed residential communities such as Arabian Ranches; and Dubailand, a sports, leisure and entertainment district that will be twice the size of Florida's Walt Disney World when completed in 2018.

But even as Dubai undergoes dramatic expansion to gear up for the millions more foreign residents, business travellers and tourists it hopes to attract in the years ahead, Dubai Creek remains the established heart and soul of the city. Dubai began on the banks of the creek, and for visitors there's no better place to begin than at the beginning.

SHINDAGHA

The historic **Shindagha** peninsula on the western bank of Dubai's tidal creek has now been swallowed by Bur Dubai, but was once a distinct settlement, separated by a wide stretch of sand known as Ghubaiba, which flooded at high tide.

A curling promontory at the mouth of the creek, Shindagha is the most likely site of the original fishing and pearling village, which would have consisted of simple palm-frond dwellings called *barasti* or *arish*, and perhaps a few mud-brick houses. The main residential area for Dubai's Arab population in the 1800s and early 1900s, Shindagha was the traditional seat of the community's leaders. It was here in 1823 that Mohammed Bin Hazza welcomed the Persia-based British Political Resident in the Gulf, Lieutenant J. McLeod. Through an interpreter, McLeod briefed Hazza on British intentions along the coast, including plans to place a representative agent in the then more established settlement of Sharjah, to the north.

It was here, too, that 800 members of the Al Bu Falasah sub-section of the Bani Yas tribe settled after seceding from

Abu Dhabi in 1833. Led by Sheikh Maktoum Bin Buti and Sheikh Obaid Bin Saeed Bin Rashid, the Bani Yas influx transformed the politics of a community that had numbered around 1,200 people before their arrival. Maktoum became its new ruler, establishing at Shindagha the Al Maktoum dynasty that rules Dubai to this day.

Heritage Museums

The Maktoum family's former home, built in 1896 for Sheikh Maktoum Bin Hasher Al Maktoum but now named after his successor Sheikh Saeed, who ruled the emirate from 1912 to 1958, was rebuilt in the 1980s and is a museum of early life in Dubai. The imposing **Sheikh Saeed Al Maktoum House** (Sat–Thur 8am–8.30pm, Fri 3–9.30pm; charge) contains photographs, an exhibition about fishing and pearling, coins, stamps and historic documents. Located on a quiet stretch of the creekside promenade, a 10-minute walk from the bustle of the Bur Dubai *abra* (water taxi) station, the two-storey structure, built of coral stone and covered in lime and sand-coloured plaster, is a fine example of late-19th-century Arabian architecture, with Persian and Islamic influences. Architectural features include arched doorways, sculpted window overhangs, vaulted high-beamed ceilings and carved trellis screens, but the over-riding feature of the house is its four *barjeel*, or wind-towers, an innovative, early form of air conditioning introduced by traders from Iran. The second-floor bedrooms and balconies above the high

Arabian architecture at Sheikh Saeed Al Maktoum House

perimeter walls offered vantage points for Sheikh Saeed, grandfather of the present ruler, and his son Sheikh Rashid, 'the Father of Dubai', to watch the sea trade moving in and out of the creek.

Today the view out to sea, across the busy road that leads to Shindagha Tunnel, one of the modern creek's five crossing points, is dominated by **Port Rashid**. Construction on this deep-water harbour began in 1967, instigated by Sheikh Rashid during an era of massive public works programmes that established an infrastructure to support the fledgling oil industry, as well as accommodate non-oil trade. With

A water taxi on the creek with the Juma Grand Mosque beyond

the opening of the 3,300-sq m (35,522-sq ft) **Dubai Cruise Terminal** at Port Rashid in 2001, the Shindagha peninsula is now a convenient first stop for cruise-ship passengers.

Port Rashid aside, Shindagha, which consisted of 250 homes at the turn of the 20th century, was neglected in the rush to develop the city in the early years of the oil boom. When Sheikh Saeed died in 1958, the Maktoums moved away. But the regeneration of this stretch of the creek, which followed the rebuilding of Sheikh Saeed's house, has seen the reconstruction of two other heritage houses, **Sheikh Joma'a Al Maktoum House**, which dates from 1928, and **Sheikh Obaid Bin Thani House**, which dates from 1916, as well as the restoration of six small mosques. It's also home now to the **Heritage and Diving villages** (Sat–Thur 8am–10pm, Fri 8–11am and 4–10pm), a short walk north of Sheikh Saeed's House.

The focus for cultural activities, music and dance during the annual Dubai Shopping Festival in January, and on public holidays, the **Heritage Village** offers a year-round glimpse of what life was like in the Emirates through the ages. On display within the compound are the camel- and goat-hair tents that nomadic *bedu*, including the Maktoums of the Bani Yas tribe, used before they settled on the coast, and houses of mud and stone that were typical of Dubai's mountain region around the inland enclave of Hatta. The nearby **Diving Village** presents a nautical variation on the heritage theme, with demonstrations and displays about pearl diving and the manufacture of fishing nets and traditional boats, which were made of palm fronds and wood.

Dhows are still used for transporting cargo

'Venice of the Middle East'

One of the most attractive features of Shindagha, however, is the view from its promenade back along the creek, past the busy *abra* stations, the waterfront at Dubai Old Souk, the Juma Grand Mosque with its impressive 70-m (231-ft) high minaret and the Emiri Diwan (or Ruler's Court), towards architect Carlos Ott's sail-shaped National Bank of Dubai building and the triangular blue wedge that is the Dubai

> ### Arabian boats
>
> The name given to wooden boats in the Arabian Gulf is *dhow*, from the Swahili word for boat, *dau*. These traditional cargo and fishing vessels are still a common sight on Dubai Creek.

Chamber Of Commerce. With the buildings crowded in on either side of the waterway, the *abras* packed with passengers criss-crossing the creek and the occasional passing *dhow* loaded with exports for Pakistan, India or East Africa, the scene is reminiscent of a Canalletto painting, recalling an old nickname for Dubai you don't often hear these days – 'Venice of the Middle East'.

BUR DUBAI

If Shindagha was the residential district of historic Dubai, with no shops or souks, then **Bur Dubai** was its central business district. It was here that the first purpose-built office building, Beit Al Wakeel, was constructed in the early 1930s to house British agents and trade missions. Here, too, stood the headquarters of the British Bank of the Middle East, the city's first bank, established in 1946.

Historically more cosmopolitan than Shindagha, Bur Dubai was home to Persian and Indian merchants who settled here with their families from 1894, when Sheikh Maktoum Bin Hasher declared free-trade status for the city,

An old *dhow* stands outside the Dubai Museum in Al Fahidi Fort

though the major influx of immigrants came after 1902, when customs duties at Lingah, on the Persian coast, were increased and Bur Dubai became a more attractive hub for trade. The Persian influence on the architecture of Bur Dubai is still evident today, in the 25 surviving wind-tower houses that make up the Bastakiya district, the only surviving cluster of such buildings on the Arabian side of the Gulf. A legacy of the early Indian influence is the Hindu Shaif temple, located in a narrow alley near the souk.

Dubai Museum

The oldest surviving structure in Bur Dubai is **Al Fahidi Fort**, which was built between 1787 and 1799 to guard the landward approach to the town. The Portuguese-influenced fortress served as the ruler's residence and the seat of government in the past, and would have been a refuge for the inhabitants of the coastal community in the event of attack.

Since 1971, the fort has housed **Dubai Museum** (Sat–Thur 8.30am–8.30pm, Fri 2.30–8.30pm; charge). The building itself – a simple, square, high-walled compound with corner towers covered in sun-baked plaster – is an arresting, though apparently care-worn, sight among the modern apartment blocks and office buildings of Al Fahidi Street. On the plaza beside it stands a stunning wooden **pearling dhow**. The surprise within is the quality of the exhibits, most of which are displayed in underground galleries. From the multi-media overview of the development of Dubai to the detailed dioramas recreating scenes from everyday life in the years before oil, the creative, contemporary presentation of its exhibits make this museum an unexpected gem. Among the artefacts displayed here are finds from the archaeological sites at Al Qusais and Jumeira, dating from the Iron Age and 6th century respectively.

Between the fort and the creek is the landmark **Juma Grand Mosque** (Muslims only), one of the oldest in Dubai, which has the tallest minaret in the city, nine large domes, 45 small domes and space for 1,200 worshippers. It was built in 1900 and rebuilt in 1998.

Pearl Diving

Before 'black gold' there were pearls. In the centuries before oil was discovered, pearling was the mainstay of the Dubai economy, involving the majority of the creek settlements' men and boys. From June to September boats of between 15 and 60 men stayed at sea for up to four months, moving from one pearl oyster bed to another and sheltering from storms on Gulf islets. Equipped with little more than a nose clip, ear plugs and finger pads, and surviving on a diet of fish and rationed water, the men would dive on weighted ropes to depths of around 15m (49ft) up to 50 times a day. In two or three minutes under water they could collect up to a dozen pearl oysters.

Pearls were graded according to their size, colour and shape. In the early 20th century, the best pearls or *jiwan* (a derivative of 'Grade One' or 'G-One') could fetch 1,500 rupees, but while Dubai's pearl merchants grew wealthy, a diver's wages for the entire season could be as little as 30–60 rupees. Famous for their rose-colouring, Dubai pearls were traded in India, from where they were sent to Paris. The popularity of the Japanese cultured pearl from the 1930s devastated the Gulf industry virtually overnight. After struggling on for another decade, the last great pearling expedition sailed from Dubai in 1949.

Bastakiya

➤ As recently as the mid-1990s **Bastakiya** was a run-down place with up to 100 people crammed into a single house. Now, thanks to a restoration programme undertaken by Dubai Municipality's Historical Buildings Section, Bastakiya has become a case study for urban conservation in the Arab world and is enjoying a new lease of life as the city's arts quarter. It played host to the emirate's first Creek Art Fair in 2008, a fringe event that ran parallel to the high-profile Art Dubai, a contemporary art exhibition.

Located on the creekside next to the Emiri Diwan, or Ruler's Palace, Bastakiya would not have been built were it not for the city's open-door policy to foreign trade. Its original residents were wealthy traders from Bastak and Lingah on the coast of modern-day Iran – hence the name. They settled here, close to their shops in the nearby Abra Souk, between 1902 and 1950, the period in which their distinctive wind-tower homes were built.

Religious Tolerance

According to the Sheikh Mohammed Centre for Cultural Understanding (see page 36), 'Cultural and religious diversity has made the Emirates probably the most open and tolerant country within the region. Dubai and the UAE in general are liberal in allowing foreigners to maintain their own religious practices and lifestyles.'

Although Emiratis are Muslims and the legal system that applies to locals and foreigners alike is based on Islamic *Sharia'h* law, the Dubai Government allows people of other faiths to gather for worship, as long as they don't proselytise Muslims. A number of Christian churches have been established on land provided by the rulers on the Bur Dubai side of the creek. As Friday is the local weekend, most churches have main services then – Sunday is a normal working day.

Bastakiya's famous wind-towers, which can rise to a height of 15m (49ft), were an early form of air conditioning – the four open sides of each square tower catching the breeze and channelling it into rooms below, which were used for meals, entertaining or sleeping in. The walls of each house were made of coral stone, which, thanks to its porous nature, has low thermal conductivity, keeping temperatures inside to a minimum. For privacy and security, there were no windows on the ground floor, just a few ventilation holes, which gives the narrow *sikka* alleyways between the brown, plaster-covered buildings an *Arabian Nights* atmosphere.

The lanes of historic Bastakiya

Wonderfully restored examples of Bastakiya's historic houses include the venerable **Majlis Gallery** (Sat–Thur 9.30am–8pm), which was founded by British expatriate Alison Collins in her family home in 1989; the **XVA Gallery** (Sat–Thur 9am–9pm), which boasts a calming courtyard coffee shop, an eclectic fashion and lifestyle boutique, S*uce, known for stocking works of avant-garde Middle Eastern designers, and guest accommodation; and **Bastakiah Nights** (tel: 04 353 7772; Sat–Thur 9am–midnight, Fri 9–11.30am and 1pm–midnight), an Arabic and Iranian restaurant that opened in 2005 in one of Bastakiya's oldest and largest houses, which was built in three phases between 1890 and 1940.

Bastakiya is also home to the **Sheikh Mohammed Centre For Cultural Understanding** (tel: 04 353 6666; Sat–Thur 9am–2pm), which organises walking tours of the district as well as guided tours of Jumeira Mosque and visits to the homes of local people, to increase awareness and understanding between cultures. Public lectures on Dubai's heritage and culture are held from time to time in another house that has been restored and turned into a lecture hall, **Dar Al Nadwa** (tel: 04 353 7373), which was originally constructed in 1925 and was restored in 2001. A stroll around Bastakiya will throw up other cultural curios, such as the **Arabic Calligraphy Museum** and a **Stamp Museum**, and photo-opportunities abound in its alleyways and plazas. Dubai Municipality's **Historical Buildings Section**, which is now based in a restored Bastakiya house, isn't a tourist attraction as such, but sightseers are welcome to step inside and view its courtyard and verandas.

Bur Dubai Souk

Known variously as the Abra Souk, Grand Souk Bur Dubai and the Textile Souk, **Bur Dubai Souk** (Sat–Thur 9am–1pm and 4–10pm, Fri 4–10pm) runs parallel to the creek below Al Fahidi Fort and Juma Grand Mosque. Among its textile shops and stalls is a forerunner of the gleaming skyscrapers on Sheikh Zayed Road – **Beit Al Wakeel**, the city's first office building. Commissioned by Sheikh Saeed in 1930 and completed soon afterwards, it was previously known as the Gray Mackenzie Building after the British company based there, the licensed shipping agents in Dubai since 1891. Restored in 1995, Beit Al Wakeel is now a 'traditional' waterfront restaurant.

Nearby, at the water's edge, **Dubai Old Souk Abra Station** is a fascinating spot to stand and watch the traffic on the creek. For one dirham you can catch an *abra*, or water taxi, from here to the Al Sabkha Abra Station on the Deira side of the creek. From the water you'll get an excellent view of the preserved buildings on the creek front. However, if you want to cross to the gold or spice souks in Deira, walk on to **Bur Dubai Abra Station**, near the entrance to Bur Dubai Souk – the *abras* that depart from here will drop you closer to the souks. Air-conditioned water taxis also operate from both stations.

For more contemporary shopping, **Al Fahidi Street** is the place for value-for-money electronics – all the major brands are represented – as well as colourful textile shops offering a wide variety of silks and fabrics from the Indian sub-continent. Further inland, Bur Dubai's main thorough-fare, **Khalid Bin Al Waleed Road**, has the city's largest concentration of computer shops, while at its junction with Sheikh Khalifa Bin Zayed Road (Trade Centre Road) stands

An *abra* (water taxi) arrives at Dubai Old Souk Station

one of Dubai's grandest malls, **BurJuman Centre** (Sat–Wed 10am–10pm, Thur–Fri 2pm–midnight), which was expanded in 2005 to incorporate Saks Fifth Avenue as a new anchor tenant. One of Dubai's most unusual sightseeing vehicles, the amphibious **Wonder Bus** (tel: 04 359 5656), departs from the BurJuman Centre.

Al Seef Road

Away from the heritage sights and the shops, **Al Seef Road**, at the creek end of Sheikh Khalifa Bin Zayed Road, is popular with fishermen, walkers and joggers. Day or night, the view from the quayside in front of the British Embassy compound across the water to Carlos Ott's 125m (410ft) **National Bank of Dubai Building** is one of the best in the city. In daylight, in particular, the bank's convex, sail-shaped glass façade reflects activity on the creek below it, and when there's dust in the air and the sun hits the glass panels at just the right angle, the building shoots off dazzling rays of light. Next to it stands the triangular blue Dubai Chamber Of Commerce. The Al Seef waterfront is the point of embarkation for **Danat Dubai Cruises** (tel: 04 351 1117) and dinner cruises on **Bateaux Dubai** (tel: 04 399 4994). Water taxis and air-conditioned Waterbuses operate out of **Al Seef Abra Station**.

DEIRA

One of the three settlements that comprised early Dubai, Deira lies across the creek from Shindagha and Bur Dubai. After settling in Shindagha in 1833, the Maktoums had to wait until 1841 before their power base extended to Deira. That same year, an outbreak of smallpox on the west side of the creek prompted many of its inhabitants to cross to Deira and settle here. The early dwellings were made of

One man and his camel

palm fronds, but after fire ravaged the community in 1894 more substantial homes were constructed, using coral stone and gypsum.

Deira's great souk, Al Souk Al Kabeer, was built in 1850. Stocked with imported goods, offloaded from *dhows* on the nearby creek, it was the largest market in the region in the second half of the 19th century. By 1908, according to the historian and geographer G.G. Lorimer, there were 1,600 houses and 350 shops in Deira, compared to 200 houses and 50 shops in Bur Dubai.

Together with Bur Dubai, Deira formed the commercial heart of Dubai, but it was also the district where new services emerged: the children of Shindagha and Bur Dubai crossed to Deira for an education after the city's first school was established here in 1912, and people came to Deira for medical treatment after the first hospital on the Trucial Coast, Al Maktoum Hospital, was established here in 1949.

The Gold Souk

Arguably the most famous attraction in Deira today is the **Gold Souk** (Sat–Thur 9.30am–1pm and 4–10pm, Fri 4–10pm), a cluster of streets shaded by a high roof in the Al Ras neighbourhood, just off Old Baladiya Street.

The third largest centre in the world for gold bullion after London and Zurich, Dubai was trading in gold long before 'black gold' was discovered. In fact, when the bottom fell out of the local pearl market in the 1930s, after the development of the cultured pearl in Japan, it was gold that saw Dubai through one of its leanest periods. Historically, it was demand from India that drove trade, and even today it's the higher-carat, orange-tinted gold favoured on the subcontinent that predominates in the souk's window displays.

Deira's Gold Souk has 700 shops

With 700 shops, Dubai Gold Souk is claimed to be the biggest in the world, and with the lowest prices, too (haggling for the 'best price' is expected). As well as intricately worked necklaces, bangles, rings, earrings and brooches in 14-, 18-, 22- and 24-carat gold, visitors might opt for a gold ingot or simple souvenir coin.

A magnet for visitors throughout the year, the souk is particularly busy during the month-long Dubai Shopping Festival in January–February, when the area becomes a focal point for the raffle draws and street entertainment that are features of the festival. The biggest draw, however, are the discounts offered by traders throughout the month.

The Spice Souk

Closer to the creek, at the intersection of Old Baladiya Street and the creekside Bani Yas Road, is Dubai's **Spice Souk** (Sat–Thur 9.30am–1pm and 4–8pm, Fri 4–8pm). Fronted by the restored heritage buildings of Deira Old Souk, just across the road from the Deira Old Souk Abra Station, the Spice Souk is smaller than it once was, but what it lacks in quantity it makes up for in atmosphere: the lanes here are much narrower, darker and more uneven than the streets of the Gold Souk and the air is scented by the colourful offerings displayed outside each shop: cloves, cardamom, cinnamon, saffron, rose petals and incense. At an undefined point, the Spice Souk becomes **Deira Old Souk**, which offers an uninspiring selection of cheap cooking utensils. This is not to be confused with **Deira Covered Souk**, which is 0.5km (550yds) or so further north along Sikkat Al Khail Road, in the Al Sabkha neighbourhood. Further down Naif Road, past the Deira Covered Souk, the Naif Souk once sold bargain textiles, costume jewellery and sewing accoutrements, but it was recently gutted in a fire. Reconstruction work is in progress.

Fresh fish in Deira's market

The Fish Market

One of the most interesting markets in the city is Deira's **Fish Market** (7am–11pm), located between Al Khaleej Road and the Gulf, and the mouth of the creek and the imposing Hyatt Regency Hotel. Although it is open throughout the day, the best time to visit is early in the morning when the market is busy with porters pushing wheelbarrows full of seafood between the refrigerated lorries and the market halls. The variety of species is fascinating, some recognisable, some not: shark, barracuda, tuna, kingfish, sea bream, red snapper, *hammour* (Gulf cod), mackerel, sardines, squid and king prawns. Near the market entrance is **Fisherman's House**, a small museum that has information and exhibits about Dubai's fishing heritage and the 350 species of fish found in UAE waters.

Deira City Centre

Continuing the shopping theme, Deira boasted Dubai's first modern mall in 1981 – Al Ghurair Centre, on Al Rigga Road, which after being refurbished is still going strong as **Al Ghurair City** (Sat–Thur 10am–10pm, Fri 2–10pm). But the best-known mall on the Deira side of Dubai Creek is undoubtedly **Deira City Centre** (Sun–Wed 10am–10pm, Thur–Sat 10am–midnight), located between the Maktoum and Garhoud bridges, opposite Dubai Creek Golf and Yacht Club. Known simply as 'City Centre', the mall has several value-for-money electronics stores – Jacky's, Jumbo and Plug-Ins – and a cluster of Arabian-themed souvenir shops in the **Arabian Treasures** area of the mall, near Woolworths: a convenient one-stop shop for regionally made carpets, pashmina shawls, Arabian perfumes, coffee sets and wooden items. The mall also has a **tourism information desk**, located on the ground floor, underneath the central escalators, and a children's entertainment centre, **Magic Planet**.

Guinness records

Dubai is associated with some 35 Guinness world records, including the largest gathering of people with the same name, set by 1,500 Mohammeds in 2005.

Al Ahmadiya School, Dubai's first, is now a museum of education

Al Ahmadiya School

There are several well-preserved historic sites in Deira. Foremost among them is **Al Ahmadiya School** (Sat–Thur 8am–7.30pm, Fri 2.30–7.30pm), which is located on Al Ahmadiya Street in the Al Ras area, a short walk from the Gold Souk. Al Ahmadiya School was the first semi-formal school in Dubai when it was established in 1912, and one of the emirate's first regular schools when formal education was introduced in 1956.

Before it was founded by local pearl merchant Ahmad Bin Dalmouk, after whom it was named, boys were taught the Koran, Arabic calligraphy and arithmetic in their own homes by a man or woman known as *Al Muttawa* – literally 'Volunteer'. With the establishment of semi-formal schools along the Trucial Coast, typically financed by pearl merchants or *Al Tawaweesh*, the curriculum expanded to include mathematics, sciences, history, literature and astronomy.

Built in three phases, Al Ahmadiya School was initially a single-storey structure with 11 classrooms and a *liwan*, or veranda, around an inner courtyard. The upper floor was added in 1920. In 1932, following the collapse of the pearl trade, and with it the local economy, the school was forced to close, but it reopened in 1937 with a government subsidy. In the 1950s, with the introduction of a formal education system, English, sociology and more science subjects were added to the curriculum and student numbers increased. By 1962, the school had 823 students – more than it could comfortably accommodate. In 1963, when it moved to a new, larger site, the original building was closed.

During its restoration by Dubai Municipality's Historical Buildings Section from 1995, authentic building materials such as coral stone, gypsum and sandalwood were used to recreate Al Ahmadiya School as its famous old boys would have known it. Among its illustrious alumni are Sheikh Rashid Bin Saeed Al Maktoum, ruler of Dubai between 1958 and 1990, and his son Sheikh Mohammed Bin Rashid Al Maktoum, the current ruler and UAE Vice-President and Prime Minister. The school opened as a museum of education in 2000.

Heritage House

Next to Al Ahmadiya School is **Heritage House** (Sat–Thur 8am–7.30pm, Fri 2.30–7.30pm), which was also restored in the mid-1990s and opened to the public in 2000. The former residence of the Bin Dalmouk family, the pearl traders who established the school, the oldest part of Heritage House dates back to 1890, when it was built for Mohammed Bin Saeed Bin Muzaina. Sheikh Ahmad Bin Dalmouk expanded the house when he assumed ownership in 1910.

Today, the 935-sq m (10,065-sq ft) building is preserved as it would have been in the 1950s. It is one of the best surviving examples of a traditional Emirati home and provides a snapshot of the social life of Dubai's wealthier inhabitants during that period. Notable features include the separate men's and women's *majlis*, or meeting rooms, where guests would sit on embroidered silk or wool pillows around the edge of a Persian-carpeted floor, drinking Arabic coffee and discussing the economic, social and political issues of the day.

Opposite Heritage House and Al Ahmadiya School, the small, single-storey building constructed in a similar style is Bin Lootah Mosque, built in 1910. Restored in 1995, the mosque is still used for prayers and is not open to the public.

Municipality Museum

The modern home of Dubai Municipality is on the creekside next to the Radisson SAS Hotel, but its former headquarters has been preserved as another of Deira's heritage buildings. Located on the edge of the Spice Souk, across Bani Yas Road from the Deira Old Souk Abra Station, the **Municipality Museum** is a simple but elegant, two-storey structure with a long wooden balcony that recalls New Orleans' French Quarter. Restored in 1999, this former local government headquarters is now a museum of municipal history.

The Municipality Museum

Dubai's most venerable landmark: the 1962 clocktower

Deira Creekside

The Deira side of the creek is much busier than the Bur Dubai waterfront thanks to the **dow wharves** that line it more or less continually from Deira Old Souk Abra Station to Maktoum Bridge. Although Dubai has two modern container ports at Port Rashid and Jebel Ali, as well as a busy international airport, traditional wooden *dhows* are still used for transporting varied cargoes of goods between Dubai and its historic trading partners in India, Pakistan and East Africa.

The activity on and around the *dhows*, which are sometimes moored up to 10 abreast, the tyres, automotive spare parts and electrical goods stacked high on the quayside without fear of theft, the weatherbeaten features of the old sailors and the timeless design of the vessels themselves make a wander along Deira's busy quays a highlight of any visit to Dubai.

Whereas Port Rashid and Jebel Ali are off limits to tourists, access is not a problem here, so you can get a much closer look at the boats. Perhaps the best place to view the fishing and cargo *dhows* and the creek skyline behind them is the purpose-built *dhow* wharfage between the triangular blue Dubai Chamber of Commerce Building and Maktoum Bridge in Riggat Al Buteen. The quays jut into the creek here, offering an interesting perspective on Carlos Ott's **National Bank of Dubai** building.

From the *dhow* wharfage, it's just a short walk inland to the stylish **Hilton Dubai Creek**, which boasts British celebrity chef Gordon Ramsay's first overseas restaurant **Verre** (daily 7pm–midnight), established in 2001. It's also a short walk to one of Dubai's oldest landmarks, **Clocktower Roundabout**, where the Maktoum Bridge traffic intersects with Al Maktoum Road. Built in 1962, the venerable clocktower features in numerous old photographs. Originally surrounded by desert, it is one of the few structures to have survived five decades of development – a rare visual reference point in the changing face of the city. Overlooking Clocktower Roundabout, the identical towers of the **Marriott Executive Apartments Complex** are connected by a skybridge that, at 74m (242ft), is the longest in the world.

Not on the creek, but just a short detour along Al Maktoum Road from Clocktower Roundabout towards Dubai International Airport, is the **Nasser Bin Abdullatif Al Serkal Building**, which is easily distinguished by its Indian-style architecture. The ground floor contains the nearest Dubai has to a motor museum: a display of historic vehicles collected by the prominent Dubai trading family Al Serkal (Sat–Wed

Flying boat days

Dubai Creek was a landing area for Imperial Airways' flying boats in the late 1930s and 1940s.

8am–1pm and 4–7.30pm, Thur 8am–2pm). Among the vehicles on display are several Model T Fords, US military Willys Jeeps and post-war American classics such as the Ford V8 Deluxe, 1957 Buick Special and Chevrolet Fleetline.

Recreational Sites

Although there are creekside walks and beaches to enjoy in Dubai, the city lacks the long coastal corniches associated with Abu Dhabi, the Qatari capital Doha or Kuwait City. But what it does have is in Deira. The short **Deira Corniche**, across the road from the Fish Market and the Hyatt Regency Hotel, is a popular spot for watching the sun set over the Arabian Gulf. The municipality has also created a short corniche in the residential area north of The Palm Deira land reclamation project, between Al Hamriya Port and Al Mamzar Beach Park.

The largest public park on the Deira side of the creek, **Al Mamzar Beach Park** (8am–11pm; Wed women and children only; charge) is near Dubai's boundary with the neighbouring emirate of Sharjah. The park, which is on a kilometre-long spit dividing the Gulf from three large lagoons, has four beaches, two swimming pools, lots of greenery, barbecue and picnic areas, children's play areas and an amphitheatre in which international children's productions are performed during January's Dubai Shopping Festival.

Also on the Deira side of the creek, between the Maktoum and Garhoud bridges and opposite the Deira City Centre mall, is **Dubai Creek Golf and Yacht Club**, which has an 18-hole championship golf course (a past venue for the European PGA Tour Dubai Desert Classic tournament) and a picturesque marina packed with luxury boats. The club has several popular venues, including **The Boardwalk** (tel: 04 295 6000; 8am–1am), a restaurant that's particularly popular in winter thanks to the boardwalk seating over the creek; and **Qd's** (6pm–2am), an open-air bar. The 225-room **Park Hyatt** hotel adjoins the club grounds.

South-east of the golf course, across Al Garhoud Road, is the **Aviation Club**, which boasts the 5,000-seat **Dubai Tennis Stadium**, venue for the women's WTA and men's ATP professional tennis tournaments, which take place in February and March respectively. Among the popular bars and restaurants in the complex are **The Cellar** (daily noon–3.30pm and 7–11.30pm); the hugely popular **Irish Village** (Fri–Tue 11am–11pm, Wed–Thur 11am–2.30am), which extends from one side of the tennis stadium to a 'village pond' complete with resident ducks; and **Century Village**, which has Lebanese, Portuguese and Japanese restaurants. The tennis stadium also houses a British-style fish and chip shop and a Costa coffee outlet.

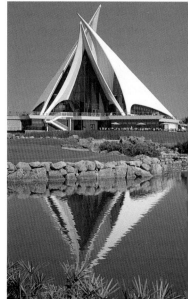

The clubhouse of the Dubai Creek Golf and Yacht Club

As well as hosting tennis legends such as Boris Becker, Andre Agassi, Martina Navratilova and Monica Seles over the years, the Aviation Club is a popular venue for concerts: Placido Domingo, Lionel Ritchie, Sting, and Bob Geldof are among the stars who have performed in the stadium since it was built in 1995, while several 1980s pop groups have made nostalgic reappearances in the Irish Village.

UMM HURAIR

Moving away from the historic centre of Dubai, there's also plenty to see and do in the districts located to the south and west of Dubai Creek. Although they are referred to locally as 'the Bur Dubai side of the creek', strictly speaking neighbourhoods such as Umm Hurair and Karama are not actually in Bur Dubai.

Creekside Park

Umm Hurair's main attraction is **Creekside Park** (8am–11pm; charge), which fronts Dubai Creek for 2.6km (1½ miles) between the Maktoum and Garhoud bridges. Together with Dubai Creek Golf and Yacht Club, on the opposite side of the waterway, the park is one of two green lungs in the centre of the city. Covering around 90 hectares

Popular with families: leafy Creekside Park in Umm Hurair

(222 acres) and containing some 280 botanical species, Creekside Park is a verdant haven for rest and recreation and a focal point for activities during national holidays and festivals. As well as a network of leafy paths for strolling, jogging, roller-blading or exploring in four-wheel cycle cars, available to rent from Gate 2, the park has an 18-hole mini-golf course, three jetties for fishing, and a 30m (98ft)-high cable car, the UAE's first.

The brightly coloured buildings of Children's City

It's also home to the vividly coloured buildings housing **Children's City** (Sat–Thur 9am–8.30pm, Fri 3–8.30pm; charge) near Gate 1, a fun, interactive learning zone and amusement facility for youngsters aged from two to 15. It houses several exhibits based around educational themes, including nature, space exploration, the human body, and local and international culture. There is also a planetarium and a special area for children under five, as well as daily educational workshops throughout the year.

Bordering the south-eastern edge of Creekside Park is an attraction for children of all ages: **WonderLand Theme and Water Park** (opening hours change throughout the year; tel: 04 324 1222/3222 to check; charge). Opened in 1996, WonderLand has 40 indoor and outdoor rides including rollercoasters and a log flume, as well as go-karting and paintballing. Its water park component is **Splashland**, which has several waterslides.

The impressive entrance to the Egyptian-themed Wafi

Al Boom Tourist Village

Between WonderLand and Garhoud Bridge is **Al Boom Tourist Village** (tel: 04 324 3000), a venue for dining – its Al Dahleez restaurant offers Arabian and international cuisine – and a point of embarkation for lunch and dinner cruises on one of nine traditional *dhows*, which ply the creek daily 2.30–4pm and 8.30–10pm.

Wafi

Shopping opportunities in Umm Hurair include the elegant **Wafi Mall** (Sat–Wed 10am–10pm, Thur–Fri 10am–midnight), part of the Egyptian-themed **Wafi** complex, which also includes the pyramid-shaped, five-star Raffles Dubai hotel; Cleopatra's Spa, regarded as one of the best in the city; nightlife venues such as Carter's, Seville's and Ginseng; and Planet Hollywood. The retail extension of Wafi offers edgy and unconventional brands. Stores such as DSquared and Kitsons attract affluent Emirati youth.

Among the mall's eateries are Wafi Gourmet, a popular Lebanese delicatessen and restaurant with balcony seating, and Elements art café, which also has balcony seating. The mall's **Encounter Zone** amusement centre offers an alternative to Children's City and WonderLand for keeping children and teenagers entertained.

Across Sheikh Rashid Road from Wafi, Dubai Police Officers' Club is where the England football team trained when they stayed in Dubai en route to the 2002 FIFA World Cup Finals in Japan.

Karama

In contrast to Wafi Mall, Al Karama – more commonly known as **Karama** – less than 2km (1 mile) away, towards Port Rashid, is one of the least exclusive, but most visited shopping destinations in Dubai. A nondescript and in places plain ugly inner-city neighbourhood of 1970s low-rise apartment buildings packed with ground-floor shops and 'ethnic' eateries, Karama is Dubai's 'bargain basement', where visitors forego the air-conditioned comfort of the modern malls to pick up brand-name goods at some of the lowest prices in the city – not to mention cheap imitations of famous clothing labels, bags and watches, the names whispered to you by hawkers as you stroll by.

Karama, Dubai's 'bargain basement'

The majority of the shops are on 18b Street, which is distinguished by the pink **Al Karama Market** building at one end – an unremarkable fish, meat, fruit and vegetable market – and the Karachi Darbar restaurant at the other, one of many inexpensive Pakistani and Indian restaurants that have earned Karama the nickname 'curry corridor'.

Karama is also home to **Dubai Central Post Office** (Sat–Thur 8am–8pm, Fri 5–9pm), on Zabeel Road, the main customs collection point for overseas packages.

SHEIKH ZAYED ROAD

The greatest concentration of landmark buildings in Dubai is on **Sheikh Zayed Road**, between Trade Centre Round-about and Interchange No. 1. From 1979 to the late-1990s, the most significant structure on this stretch of the highway was the white, 39-storey, 149-m (489-ft) **Dubai World Trade Centre** building, which features on the country's Dhs100 banknote. It was once the tallest building in the Middle East.

Today, this once most prized business address has been overtaken both in terms of physical height and prestige by the iconic **Emirates Towers**, completed in 2000, which

The towering skyscrapers
of Sheikh Zayed Road

consist of a 355-m (1,163-ft) office tower – at one point the tallest building in the Middle East and Europe – and the 309-m (1,014-ft) Jumeirah Emirates Towers Hotel, one of the tallest hotels in the world, owned by the Dubai-based Jumeirah chain (which also owns the iconic Burj Al Arab a few kilometres along the coast).

Visitors who aren't staying at Jumeirah Emirates Towers or who have no business with the blue-chip companies based in the office tower should head there anyway for a closer look at Hong Kong architect Hazel Wong's slender triangular towers, which are clad in silver aluminium with copper and silver reflective glass. 'The twin towers were conceived as pure sculptural elements, evocative of the circle and triangular geometries of the Islamic cultural vocabulary,' Wong told Dubai's *identity* magazine. She likens their positioning to 'a dance, a *pas de deux* in which the building facades capture the changing light of the desert sun and show off the dramatic integrated illumination at nightfall'. Inside the hotel, there's a stunning 30-storey atrium. The glass elevators that whisk guests to one of the highest restaurants in the Middle East, **Vu's** (Sat–Thur 12.30–3pm and 7.30pm–midnight) on the 50th floor, or the separate **Vu's Bar** (daily 6pm–3am) on the 51st floor, offer fabulous views of the Jumeira coast, as do the venues.

Between the hotel and the office tower is **Emirates Towers Boulevard**, which pips Wafi Mall for exclusivity. Among the Cartier, Emporio Armani and Pucci boutiques are two notable restaurants: the Noodle House (noon–midnight), which offers an Asian fusion menu, and Al Nafoorah (12.30–4pm and 8pm–midnight), one of the best Lebanese restaurants in the city, which has outdoor seating in winter. At lunchtime, Dubai's ruler, Sheikh Mohammed, and his entourage can often be seen in one or the other, as his Executive Office is based in the office tower.

Amazing Architecture

Other notable buildings on the Emirates Towers side of Sheikh Zayed Road include **The Tower**, a 243m (796ft) high rise, covered in blue glass with Islamic-styling and a distinctive pointed tip, which was completed in 2002. Nearer Interchange No. 1 is the 269m (883ft) **21st Century Tower**, one of the world's tallest all-residential buildings. Overlooking Interchange No. 1 is the 153m (502ft) **Dusit Dubai** hotel. Its distinctive architecture – two blue glass towers on either side of a hollow centre and joined at the upper floors – is said to resemble the traditional Thai greeting of two hands pressed together.

On the Arabian Gulf side of the highway is the imposing edifice of the Art Deco-influenced 200m (656ft) **Shangri-La Hotel**, completed in 2003; the 250m (820ft) blue and white **Chelsea Tower**, completed in 2005, which has a distinctive square opening on the top that's bisected by a vertical 40m (131ft) needle; and the 153m (501ft) **Fairmont** hotel, completed in 2002, which is topped by four glass pyramid turrets.

An airline tower

The 55-storey 21st Century Tower is entirely leased by the Emirates airline, which uses it to accommodate its flight attendants.

Just west of Interchange No. 1, a new city within a city is being developed: **Downtown Burj Dubai** features one of the world's largest shopping malls, The Dubai Mall; an 'Old Town' of traditional-style buildings; and various commercial and residential buildings, not the least of which is **Burj Dubai**, which on 21 July 2007 became the tallest building in the world and on completion is expected to stand at 818m (2,684ft). The spiralling building, based on the geometry of a desert flower and incorporating Islamic patterning, will house the world's first Giorgio Armani Hotel and residences.

Dubai's new financial district, **Dubai International Financial Centre** (DIFC), lies behind the Sheikh Zayed Road high rises on the Emirates Towers side of the highway and is home to some of the world's most exclusive private investment banks and a host of luxury boutiques, including Villa Moda, a number of art galleries and hip grooming salons. Nearer Trade Centre Roundabout, the exhibition halls at **Dubai International Exhibition Centre** host the biennial Middle East International Motor Show and a number of other international trade shows and events.

The Sheikh Zayed Road skyline between Trade Centre Roundabout and Interchange No. 1 has already attracted

Burj Dubai, the tallest building in the world

Hollywood's attention: it makes an appearance in the thriller *Code 46*, starring Tim Robbins and Samantha Morton, and provides a hazy backdrop for the fictional Gulf state in *Syriana*, starring George Clooney and Matt Damon. Perhaps the best place to view it is from the venerable Dubai World Trade Centre, which has a viewing platform on the 36th floor.

On misty mornings, when the traffic on Sheikh Zayed Road is fog-bound, the tops of the taller buildings appear through the cloud, creating the floating 'cloud city' effect that appears in postcard images. Gaining access to the DWTC's viewing platform is far from straightforward, however. Visitors who turn up on spec should speak to a security guard in the tower's ground-floor reception, who might arrange an escort. Alternatively, an appointment can be made in advance by contacting the World Trade Centre's Property Manager (tel: 04 309 7009).

The vast Dubai International Exhibition Centre

Café Culture

Sheikh Zayed Road's high-rise hotels – Emirates Towers, Dusit Dubai, Shangri-La, Towers Rotana, Crowne Plaza and Fairmont – offer a variety of restaurants and nightspots, but on street level there are numerous eateries and coffee shops that make refreshing pit stops during a tour of the city. On the Emirates Towers side is the hip **Cosmo** (daily 7am–1am) in The Tower, which has an international menu and *shisha* terrace; the chintzy Victoriana-inspired **Shakespeare and Co** (daily 7am–12.30am) in the Al Attar Business Tower; and **Japengo Café** (daily 7.30am–12.30am) in the Oasis Tower, which offers an international menu with an Asian fusion twist. For delicious Arabic food try the Lebanese **Automatic** (daily noon–1am) in Jumeirah Tower; or **Al Safadi** (Sat–Thur 10am–2am, Fri 8am–2am) in Al Kawakeb Building A. For authentic Japanese dishes served up in a no-nonsense Japanese high street-style eatery, complete with racks of Manga comic books, Sumo wrestling on TV and Japanese salarymen slurping noodles at the counter, try **Bentoya Kitchen** (Sat–Thur noon–3pm and 6.30–11.30pm, Fri 5–11pm) at the back of Al Kawakeb Building D, towards Interchange No. 1.

Highlights on the Arabian Gulf side of Sheikh Zayed Road include the Japanese **Wagamama** (daily noon–midnight) in the Crowne Plaza; South African chicken chain **Nando's** (daily noon–2am) in Saeed Tower II; and the European **Bocadillo** (Sat–Thur 11am–2am, Fri noon–2am), in the side of Khalid Al Attar Tower. Options for Lebanese cuisine include the fashionable **Olive House** (daily 8am–1am), next to Starbucks in Tower No. 1, and **Byblos** (daily 7am–midnight) in Al Durrah Tower.

Also on Sheikh Zayed Road, further towards Abu Dhabi, on the desert side of the highway near Interchange No. 4, are the **Gold and Diamond Park** with its jewellery outlets, museum and manufacturing units, and **Mall of the Emirates**. The

The Mall of the Emirates contains 400 shops – and a ski slope

Emirates and **Montgomerie** golf clubs are on the desert side of the highway near Interchange No. 5, while **Ibn Battuta Mall** is on the desert side of the highway near Interchange No. 6 in Jebel Ali.

Marvellous Malls

Both Mall of the Emirates and The Dubai Mall are spectacular shopping destinations. The former, located in the largely residential Al Barsha district, is distinguished by the large indoor ski slope that coils around the exterior architecture: **Ski Dubai** (Sun–Wed 10am–11pm, Thur 10am–midnight, Fri 9am–midnight, Sat 9am–11pm; charge) is the first indoor ski resort in the Middle East, with five runs and the world's largest indoor Snow Park, where it's possible to have a snowball fight even when the mercury is touching 48°C (118°F) outside. Mall of the Emirates is also home to **Dubai Community Theatre and Arts Centre** (tel: 04 341 4777). In the Downtown Burj

Dubai development is The Dubai Mall – one of the world's largest shopping malls with the added attractions of an aquarium and an ice-skating rink as well as iconic department stores like Galeries Lafayette and Bloomingdale's.

On the Arabian Gulf side of Sheikh Zayed Road is the lush **Safa Park** (daily 8am–11pm; Tue women only; charge) near Interchange No. 2, a popular venue for walkers and joggers; and, opposite Emirates golf course near Interchange No. 5, the information-technology free-zone **Dubai Internet City** and the **Hard Rock Café**, which is currently closed for renovation.

THE JUMEIRA COAST

If there is one district that has become synonymous with Dubai's emergence as a beach holiday destination in recent years it's the coastal district of Jumeira, which is sometimes spelt 'Jumeirah', most commonly in company names such as the Jumeirah group, which not only owns landmark hotels in Dubai, but also the Carlton Tower and Lowndes hotels in London, and the Essex House hotel, which overlooks New York's Central Park.

With or without the 'h', there's actually much more to Jumeira than just Jumeira: the world-famous coastline commonly referred to as 'Jumeira Beach' starts in Jumeira, sure enough, but significant portions of it are actually in the districts of Umm Suqeim and Al Sufouh. Strictly speaking, Jumeira's most famous landmark, the 321-m (1,053-ft) Burj Al Arab hotel is in Umm Suqeim not Jumeira, while

Coastal growth

Dubai's natural coastline is 72km (45 miles) long, but land reclamation projects are extending it by an incredible 1,500km (932 miles), which is longer than the natural coastline of the entire UAE.

The Palm Jumeirah (with an 'h'), one of the engineering wonders of the modern world, lies off the coast of Al Sufouh. That said, since 'Jumeira' is the name most commonly associated with the Dubai coastline southwest of the creek, stretching from Port Rashid to Jebel Ali, we shall consider all attractions that fall within that area in this section.

Jumeira's main artery is Jumeira Road, which runs for some 15km (9 miles) from Union House near Dubai Dry Docks to the Madinat Jumeirah resort, after which the coast road towards more luxury hotels and Dubai Marina is Al Sufouh Road. As with the name of the district, Jumeira's main highway suffers from an identity crisis, with 'Beach Road' and even 'The Jumeira Strip' sometimes used instead of 'Jumeira Road'. Lying between Jumeira Road and Sheikh Zayed Road, roughly parallel to both, is Al Wasl Road. When traffic is heavy on Jumeira Road, as it

Lifeguards keep an eye on the Jumeira coast

can be around Mercato Mall on Thursday evenings, Al Wasl Road provides an alternative route, and vice versa.

Jumeira Mosque

The first taste of Jumeira for many visitors will be the hotel they are staying in: from Dubai Marine Beach Resort and Spa nearest the city centre to the Sheraton Jumeira Beach Resort & Towers near Jebel Ali, some 23km (14 miles) away, the Jumeira coast boasts the finest resort hotels in the Arabian Gulf. When it comes to sightseeing, however, one of the first stops for organised tours is **Jumeira Mosque**, on the city end of Jumeira Road. Built of stone in the medieval Fatimid-style between 1975 and 1978, Jumeira Mosque is the only one in the city that non-Muslims are permitted to enter: the Sheikh Mohammed Centre for Cultural Understanding (tel: 04 353 6666) arranges tours on Sundays and Thursdays, starting at 10am.

Union House, a modest, round, glass-walled structure where the ruling sheikhs of six emirates declared the UAE a independent federation on 2 December 1971 (the seventh emirate, Ras Al Khaimah joined in 1972) is a short walk from Jumeira Mosque towards Dubai Dry Docks – look for the giant flagpole and UAE flag that's above it.

Along Jumeira Road

The area around Jumeira Mosque, with its myriad cafés and small malls, is the nearest Dubai has to an urban village. As Jumeira was the closest coastal suburb to the city, it was here that many expatriates settled in the 1960s, '70s and '80s, when the nickname 'Jumeira Jane' became synonymous with a certain type of expat wife who spent her days tanning by the pool of a private club and lunching with friends. Although many long-term expats have taken advantage of property laws introduced in 2002 allowing them to buy their own

Jumeira Mosque, one of Dubai's most photographed sites

homes further afield, in Emirates Hills and Dubai Marina, Jumeira is still a popular place for social gatherings, day or night. Across the road from Jumeira Mosque, Palm Strip Mall has the original **Japengo Café** (there are others on Sheikh Zayed Road, in Souk Madinat Jumeirah and at Ibn Battuta Mall) and a Starbucks, while just a short walk away on the mosque side of the road is the very popular **Lime Tree Café** (daily 7.30am–6pm), another Dubai original that has birthed a second outlet at Ibn Battuta Mall.

Continuing west along Jumeira Road, **Magrudy's Mall** is home to the original Magrudy's book shop (the chain now extends to Deira City Centre, BurJuman Centre, Festival City and Ibn Battuta Mall) and the coffee shop **Gerard**, a Dubai institution that has survived the influx of American and European franchise cafés and is particularly popular with young Emiratis. Next door, in the **Jumeirah Centre**, **La Brioche** café attracts a cosmopolitan clientele with its excellent-value meals and friendly service. The next mall along, **Jumeira Plaza**, has a **Dôme** café that's also popular with locals and expats alike. The **Beach Centre**, a kilometre or so further on, has an **Automatic** restaurant, serving authentic Lebanese food. Across the road from Jumeira Plaza is **The Village Mall**, which boasts another of Dubai's popular Victoriana-inspired **Shakespeare and Co** cafés, with outdoor seating in winter. There are also a number of fast-food outlets in the area.

Further south-west along Jumeira Road is the Italian-inspired **Mercato Mall** (Sat–Thur 10am–10pm, Fri 2–10pm), whose faux Tuscan and Venetian architecture has made it a tourist attraction in its own right. Inside, the large central atrium, with its glass roof, old clock, coffee shop and escalators, resembles a 19th-century railway station. As well as designer-label stores, a Virgin Megastore and seven-screen cinema, the first floor has a cluster of shops selling carpets and regional handicrafts. Various options for food in the mall include the Bella Donna Italian restaurant on the first floor, which has outdoor balcony seating with sea views, and the popular ground-floor bakery and café Paul, which recreates the alfresco experience indoors in its own 'market square'.

Arts Venues

The next mall along Jumeira Road, **Town Centre**, has Café Céramique (daily 8am–midnight), where diners can satisfy their creative urges by painting crockery of various shapes and sizes as they munch on lunch. The café specialises in bagels and offers a pleasing sea view from its first-floor balcony. Amateur artists should return for their painted crockery a few days later, when it has been glazed.

The Creative Art Centre

Sticking with the artistic theme, the **Creative Art Centre** (Sat–Thur 8am–6pm) is located in a converted villa on Street 77, just a short walk along Jumeira Road from Town Centre. As well as selling framed Arabian-themed pictures and maps, the centre is a treasure trove packed with antiques, jewellery, ceramics and wooden items from the UAE and Oman. A more traditional arts venue, showcasing work by artists from around the world, is the **Green Art Gallery** (Sat–Thur 10am–9pm) in a converted villa on Street 51, behind Dubai Zoo. Across the road from Town Centre, **Dubai International Art Centre** (tel: 04 344 4398; Sun–Wed 8.30am–7pm, Sat and Thur 8.30am–4pm) runs various courses and displays work by local artists.

If painting crockery isn't enough to keep the children entertained, **Dubai Zoo** (Wed–Mon 10am–5pm; charge), located between Jumeira Plaza and Mercato Mall, has some 1,200 animals, including lions, tigers, giraffes, monkeys and bears. However, this once private collection and refuge for exotic animals illegally smuggled into Dubai has outgrown its decades-old Jumeira home, and the animals are living in poor conditions. Plans to relocate the zoo to a larger site have been shelved for the time being.

Best Beaches

Alternatively, of course, there's the beach. While Jumeira has many luxury hotels that restrict beach access to guests, there are still a number of free public beaches along the coast. The one with the best facilities – shaded seating, toilets, showers and nearby refreshment stalls – is **Jumeira Open Beach**, next to Dubai Marine Beach Resort and Spa and behind The Village Mall. Bathers should beware, however: while the waters may look calm, Jumeira has notoriously strong rip tides that can drag even experienced swimmers out to sea. While swimming trunks and bikinis are acceptable on the beach, bathers should cover up for visits to the cafés and malls on nearby Jumeira Road.

Sumptuous hotels line Jumeira's sandy beaches

Another popular free beach is on the city side of the Burj Al Arab hotel, which is reached by turning right at the intersection of Jumeira Road and Al Thanya Street. The view of the world's tallest hotel from this stretch of beach is stunning, particularly at sunset. Alternatively, for a nominal entrance charge, **Jumeirah Beach Park** (daily 8am–11pm; Sat women and children only; charge) combines a public beach with the features of a resort hotel, including lawns and lush greenery, lifeguards and refreshment areas. There are also areas for barbecuing your own food.

Heritage Sites

Inland from Jumeirah Beach Park, a residential neighbourhood between Jumeira Road and Al Wasl Road is the unlikely location of one of the Arabian Gulf's most significant archaeological sites: the **Jumeira Archaeological Site** (Sun–Thur 7.30am–2.30pm), where the ruins of a port town dating back more than 1,000 years have been uncovered by archaeologists since 1969. The original settlement, strategically positioned on the ancient trade route between Mesopotamia and Oman, dates back to the pre-Islamic Sassanid era, which ended in the 7th century AD. The site was built upon and expanded by the Abbasids in the first two or three centuries of the Islamic era and is today one of the largest and most important early Islamic sites in the Gulf. Among the excavated ruins are the foundations of several houses, including the Sassanid-era governor's palace, market buildings, a large caravanserai in which travellers would meet and do business, and a small mosque.

Jumeira's other site of historic interest is the more recent **Majlis Ghorfat Umm Al Sheif** (Sat–Thur 7.30am–2.30pm), Sheikh Saeed's modest two-storey summer resort made of coral stone and gypsum. Built in 1955, when this part of the coast was far removed from the city on the creek, the *majlis* was also used by Sheikh Rashid, father of the current ruler, before becoming a police station for a time in the 1960s. A small museum now, the grounds have an example of the traditional *falaj* system of irrigation and a *barasti* (palm frond) structure with a working wind-tower. It is located on Street 17, off Jumeira Road – look for the brown heritage-site signs between Jumeirah Beach Park and Burj Al Arab.

Umm Suqeim

Without a doubt, the jewel of the Dubai coast is **Burj Al Arab** hotel (literally 'Tower of the Arabs'), the city's best-known landmark, which since its opening in December 1999 has gained the iconic status of a Big Ben or an Eiffel Tower. The 321-m (1,053-ft) structure, shaped like a sail to complement the 'wave' design of the nearby Jumeirah Beach Hotel, dominates the surrounding residential neighbourhood and can be seen from virtually any point on the Dubai coast. A seven-star hotel, built on its own man-made island and comprising 202 two-storey suites, each with its own butler, Burj Al Arab restricts access to hotel guests or those who have booked a table at one of its restaurants. These include the fabulous Al Muntaha (literally 'The Highest'), 200m (656ft) above the Arabian Gulf with breathtaking views of the coast.

Best viewed from the public beach to the north or from the beach of the Mina A'Salam hotel at the Madinat Jumeirah resort, the most distinctive feature of 'the Burj' is the double-skinned, Teflon-coated, woven glass-fibre screen facade, which is white by day and illuminated by coloured lights at night. The space-age helicopter pad jutting out from the top floor like a mini *Starship Enterprise* was famously used

The unmistakeable Burj Al Arab

as a practice driving range by Tiger Woods and a tennis court by Roger Federer and Andre Agassi. Other notables to have stayed in the Dhs6,500-a-night suites include Hollywood stars Brad Pitt and Angelina Jolie.

Below the towering Burj Al Arab, next to the Jumeirah Beach Hotel, is **Wild Wadi Water Park** (Nov–Feb 10am–6pm, Mar–May and Sept–Oct 10am–7pm, June–Aug 10am–8pm; charge), which has 30 rides and attractions, including the Jumeirah Sceirah, the tallest free-fall slide outside North America, and the Wipeout

Flow Rider surf pool, where budding surfers can ride a continuously breaking 3-m (10-ft) high wave. The larger-than-life cartoon characters that inhabit the long-lost 'village' in the *wadi* (dry river bed) are an additional attraction for children and will happily pose for photos.

A stone's throw south along the coast, the splendid **Madinat Jumeirah** (literally 'Jumeirah City') resort takes its inspiration from the wind-tower houses of Bastakiya, but modern construction techniques allow for taller, more impressive structures, making the resort a fabulous reinterpretation of traditional Arabian architecture. A definite 'must see' for any visitor, Madinat Jumeirah, which opened in 2004, has two luxury hotels – Mina A'Salam (literally 'Port of Peace') and Al Qasr ('The Castle'), both of which have jaw-droppingly beautiful interior décor and a number of licensed restaurants and bars in idyllic sea-view settings that are open to non-guests *(see pages 129–30, 131 and 139)*.

Brand New Old

The Madinat Jumeirah resort on the Jumeira coast, completed in 2004, is a re-imagining of what Dubai could have looked like in previous centuries if builders of those times had access to modern construction materials and techniques, not to mention larger budgets. It mixes the wind-tower houses of the creekside Bastakiya heritage district with the modest former palace in Shindagha and the souks of old Dubai, and stretches them upwards and outwards. Designer Thanu Boonyawatana likened his approach to that of a movie special-effects wizard who, with the aid of computer-generated imagery, is able to recreate ancient Greece or Rome for cinema audiences: 'We thought, "What if in ancient UAE or ancient Oman they had the money we have now and the technology we have now? What would they have built?" We built what they might have built with the resources available to us.'

Madinat Jumeirah resort: 21st-century luxury in traditional style

It also has a delightful covered market, **Souk Madinat Jumeirah** (daily 10am–11pm), which despite its recent construction manages to convey an authentic atmosphere. As well as various antiques shops, clothing boutiques and handicraft stalls, the souk has a number of bars, licensed restaurants and cafés that spread onto picturesque terraces, and one of Dubai's best wine bars, The Agency.

There is also a small art gallery, Gallery One, which showcases paintings, mixed-media art and photography by local and international artists; past exhibitors include the iconic 1960s photographer Terry O'Neill. A network of canals, serviced by *abra* water taxis for guest-use only, links the hotels and Al Qasr's 29 wind-tower summer houses with the souk and various waterfront restaurants. Madinat Jumeirah also has a grand theatre and a large exhibition hall, which has hosted the likes of Bjorn Borg and John McEnroe in exhibition tennis tournaments. Madinat Jumeirah provides an opulent setting for the Dubai International Film Festival in December, which serves as a cultural bridge between film-makers and stars from Hollywood, Bollywood and the Middle East film industry.

Al Sufouh

South-west along Al Sufouh Road, **One&Only Royal Mirage** is another hotel that conjures up the atmosphere of the ancient East through arabesque architecture and styling. It too has a number of licensed restaurants and a popular nightclub, Kasbar. Scenes from the Hollywood film *Syriana* were shot here. Among the other luxury hotels on this stretch of the coast, the Andalusian-influenced **Ritz-Carlton** stands out as a stylish venue for a quiet afternoon tea on a sea-facing balcony.

Two recent developments that dominate this stretch of coast are The Palm Jumeirah and Dubai Marina. Visible from space, **The Palm Jumeirah**, is one of three ambitious palm-tree shaped land-reclamation projects off the Dubai coast. When complete, it will include some 30 hotels and resorts, including US billionaire Donald Trump's The Palm Trump International Hotel, and the themed 2,000-room Atlantis resort, which houses the exclusive Nobu restaurant. Celebrities who have bought homes on The Palm include the English footballers David Beckham and Michael Owen, and Bollywood star Shah Rukh Khan.

The high-rise buildings surrounding **Dubai Marina** can be seen for kilometres along the coast. The quayside below the residential Dubai Marina Towers is a popular spot for a late-afternoon stroll. The development's landmark hotel is Le Meridien's five-star Grosvenor House, which offers stunning views of The Palm from its upper floors and is the Dubai home of France's famous Buddha Bar restaurant and nightclub as well as Michelin-starred chef Gary Rhodes' restaurant Rhodes

Mezzanine. Jumeirah Beach Residence, a huge cluster of high-rise apartments in Dubai Marina featuring a number of beach-side cafés, boutiques and art galleries, is fast becoming a popular hang-out among locals and tourists alike.

The coastal waters near Dubai Marina, known locally as Mina Seyahi, are the stage for two UIM Class I World Powerboat Championship races hosted by Dubai International Marine Club in November–December. In March, the Dubai International Boat show pulls in top names in the luxury yacht business, such as Azimut and Ferretti. Other crowd-pulling events along Al Sufouh Road include the annual jazz festival and open-air pop concerts at **Dubai Media City** in the winter months. Among the international acts to have performed here are Sting and Fergie. Dubai Media City is also the regional base for international broadcasters and news agencies, including CNN, BBC World and Reuters.

Dubai Marina at night

AWAY FROM THE COAST

Camel Racecourse

Away from the creek and the coast, Dubai has much to attract visitors. **Nad Al Sheba**, a 10-minute drive along Route 66 from Wafi Mall in Umm Hurair or along Doha Street from Interchange No. 1, is home to Dubai's **Camel Racecourse**. Races are held on Thursdays and Fridays in winter, but throughout the year it is possible to see racing camels in training. The best times to view them as they walk in long lines between their stables on one side of the road and the training track on the other are early in the morning or late in the afternoon. The numerous camel trains are reminiscent of ancient camel caravans, and with the Sheikh Zayed Road skyline in the background, photo opportunities abound.

Nad Al Sheba

Nad Al Sheba is best known for horse racing, however. **Nad Al Sheba Racecourse** is home to the US$21.25-million Dubai World Cup in March, the richest racing event in the world and one of the most glamorous sporting and social occasions on the Dubai calendar. The Dubai World Cup trophy, made by the British Crown Jewellers Garrard and one of the largest racing trophies in the world, stands 74cm (29 ins) tall, is covered in 18-carat gold plate and weighs 5.2kg (11lb 7oz). It is on permanent display in **The Godolphin Gallery** (Nov–Apr daily 9am–5pm) behind the racecourse grandstands. The gallery, which is closed as it prepares to relocate to new premises in 2010, is a museum of the Godolphin racing stable, established in 1994 by members of Dubai's ruling Maktoum family. Among the legendary horses commemorated here are Dubai Millennium and Lammtarra – winner of the Epsom Derby, the King George VI and Queen Elizabeth Diamond Stakes at Ascot and the French Prix de l'Arc de Triomphe in 1995. Movie fans may recognise the back of the racecourse's Millennium Grandstand: it doubled as a Chinese hospital for the Hollywood movie *Code 46*, which was partly filmed in Dubai in 2003.

Continuing the equestrian theme, Nad Al Sheba is also home to the **Emirates Riding Centre**, the venue for the world's richest showjumping event, the three-day Al Maktoum Memorial Challenge Dubai International Horse Show in January, supported by Princess Haya Bint Al Hussein, the daughter of the late King Hussein of Jordan and wife of Dubai's ruler, Sheikh Mohammed. Nearby, on Muscat Street, the **Falcon and Heritage Sports Centre** (daily 10am–11pm) has several falcon dealers and shops catering to the traditional but still very popular sport of falconry, passed down from ancient *bedu* hunters. It's the best place in Dubai for a close look at these birds of prey. For more information on falcons, *see page 77.*

Racing camels exercise year-round at Nad Al Sheba

Wildlife Sanctuary

Peregrine falcons have a new role: hunting pigeons

Close to Nad Al Sheba, the tidal lagoon at the top of Dubai Creek is home to the UAE's largest bird sanctuary, **Ras Al Khor Wildlife Sanctuary**, which can host up to 15,000 birds on a single winter's day, including between 1,000 and 1,500 migrant greater flamingos *(Phoenicopterus ruber)*, which have been a protected species here since 1985. Other species that can be seen from the purpose-built viewing hides on Route 66 and Ras Al Khor Road (Route 44) include Socotra cormorants, cream-coloured coursers and crab plovers.

Along Emirates Road

Inland from Al Barsha, the Arabian Ranches property development on Emirates Road (Route 311) is home to **Dubai Polo and Equestrian Club**, which hosts international polo exhibition matches in the winter months. Arabian Ranches also has Dubai's only desert golf course, the par-72 **Desert Course**, designed by Ian Baker-Finch and Nicklaus Design. **Dubai Autodrome**, a 5.39-km (3.3-mile) Formula One-standard motor-racing circuit, is next to Arabian Ranches on Emirates Road. A venue for rounds of the FIA GT Championship, the circuit also hosts pop concerts: Phil Collins and Shakira have performed here.

Also on Emirates Road is **Global Village**, a combination of funfair and international retail park, with numerous

European, African and Asian nations represented by elaborate pavilions. A spin-off of the annual Dubai Shopping Festival in January, Global Village is open each evening from November to February.

Arising from the desert around Arabian Ranches, Dubai Autodrome and Global Village is the ambitious **Dubailand** project, which is set to become the biggest tourism, leisure and entertainment attraction in the world when the last phase is completed by 2018. Billed as a cross between Las Vegas and Orlando, Dubailand will consist of six individual themed 'worlds'. Among the attractions will be one of the world's largest shopping malls, Mall of Arabia; Dubai Sports City, complete with world-class stadia, a Manchester United soccer school and an Ernie Els-designed golf course; a Universal Studios theme park; and a number of themed hotels.

New Millennium Falcons

The fastest creature on the planet has been trained for hunting in Arabia for thousands of years, but in the 21st century the ancient skill of falconry has been maintained for sport rather than survival. Before weapons, peregrine falcons – which can achieve speeds of 320kph (199mph) in a dive – were used by *bedu* hunters to catch food. Wild falcons were caught and trained in two or three weeks at the start of the hunting season in October. Favoured prey was the houbara bustard, a desert bird the size of a heron whose meat could be vital to a family's survival. At the end of the season, in March, the falcon would be freed.

Today, falcons are no longer captured, but reared from hatchings. Even so, they require human contact on a daily basis, or else they become wild and unreliable. Especially keen falconers fly to Pakistan for hunting expeditions, their falcons travelling on their own special passports. Falcons are also put to practical use: Dubai's Burj Al Arab hotel employs a falconer to keep pigeons – and pigeon droppings – off the landmark property.

DAY TRIPS

The Desert

 A trip into the **desert** is highly recommended for all visitors to Dubai. The dunes that begin on the outskirts of the city continue into Abu Dhabi Emirate and eventually merge with the fabled Rub Al Khali, or Empty Quarter, the largest sand desert in the world. But visitors needn't travel far from Dubai to experience towering dunes. Less than an hour's drive along the highway to Hatta, 50km (31 miles) from the city, is a cluster of small activity centres that offer quad biking and camel rides. To venture further off road, however, an organised tour is the best option.

Several companies offer morning or late-afternoon excursions into the desert or along dry river beds known as *wadi*s in rugged 4x4 vehicles *(see page 83)*. Popular destinations include the Dubai Desert Conservation Reserve, where the Al Maha eco resort is located and in which herds of rare Arabian oryx roam free; 'Big Red', a mammoth dune that gets its name from the red iron oxide in the sand; Fossil Rock, where the fossils of marine creatures can be found on a rocky outcrop, confirming that this area was once the ocean floor; and Hatta Pools, cool mountain springs in the foothills of the Hajar range near the UAE border with Oman.

Hatta

The Dubai enclave of **Hatta**, on the highway 115km (71 miles) from the city, can be reached by hire car in around an hour. Hatta's appeal lies in the contrast of its oasis greenery and rugged mountain backdrop, but its main visitor attraction is undoubtedly **Hatta Heritage Village** (Sat–Thur 8.30am– 8.30pm, Fri 2.30–8.30pm), which traces the history of the settlement from its formation some 3,000 years ago to the 19th century and has examples of 30 traditional structures, from a

Hatta Heritage Village, built around an ancient settlement

fortress built by Sheikh Maktoum Bin Hasher Al Maktoum in 1896 to small mountain dwellings that wouldn't look out of place on the islands off the Scottish coast. The defensive watchtowers on either side of the heritage village offer superb views of the museum and the modern town. No day trip to Hatta would be complete without a refreshing drink, or perhaps a meal, beside the pool at the **Hatta Fort Hotel**, a popular weekend destination among Dubai's expatriate community.

Sharjah

On the coast north of Dubai lies **Sharjah**, once the most important town on the Trucial Coast, but now overshadowed by its more glamorous neighbour. Nevertheless, Sharjah, which was named Unesco Cultural Capital of the Arab World in 1998, has a number of attractions that make braving the traffic there worthwhile. Among them are the Central or **Blue Souk**, which has a number of carpet and handicrafts shops on the first floor; the creekside **heritage area**, with its myriad small museums, souk, art galleries and reconstructed fortress museum; and the aviation-themed **Al Mahatta Museum** (Sat–Thur 8am–8pm, Fri 4–8pm; charge), on the site of the former airport established in 1932 to serve the pioneering Imperial Airways route between Croydon and Australia. Built to protect Imperial Airways passengers from marauding *bedu*, the fortress that houses the museum was the UAE's first hotel and part of a later Royal Air Force base. As well as aircraft exhibits, including a DC3 and Avro Anson of the Gulf Aviation Company, the museum has an excellent exhibition on flight developed by the National Museums and Galleries of Wales. Located among the tall buildings on King Abd Al Aziz Street (once the main runway), a short taxi ride from the Blue Souk, it's hard to believe that the museum site was an airport as recently as 1976.

Northern Emirates

Continuing north, there are interesting fortress museums in **Ajman** (Sat–Thur 9am–1pm and 4–7pm; charge) and **Umm Al Qaiwain** (Sat, Sun, Tue–Thur 8am–1pm and 5–8pm, Fri 5–8pm; charge). Right of the highway north of Umm Al Qaiwain to Ras Al Khaimah are the ruins of **Ad-Dour**, believed to be the pre-Islamic city of Omana, known to Strabo and Pliny The Elder. Also north of Umm Al Qaiwain, **Dreamland Aqua Park** (daily Mar–May 10am–7pm, June–Oct 10am–9pm, Nov–Feb 10am–6pm; charge) is a popular alternative to Dubai's Wild Wadi, with 25 water rides and go-karting. **Ras Al Khaimah** (ancient Julfar, the birthplace of Vasco da Gama's navigator Ahmad Bin Majed) also has a fortress museum (Sat–Mon, Wed, Thur 8am–noon and 4–7pm, Fri 4–7pm; charge) and is the gateway to the mountainous Musandam Peninsula in Oman.

The East Coast

On the east coast of the UAE, between one and two hours' drive from Dubai, the highway from Masafi to Fujairah passes **Bithnah Fort**, which in its mountain oasis setting is reminiscent of the great forts of northern Oman. **Fujairah** also has an imposing fortress with a mountain backdrop. The fort, attacked by British forces in colonial times, is believed to be the oldest in the UAE, the main part dating back 500 years.

The UAE's oldest mosque, built around 1446, is on the coast 38km (24 miles) north of Fujairah at **Badiyah** (*see picture on page 19*; non-Muslims are welcome). A short drive further north is **Le Meridien Al Aqah Beach Resort**, a popular weekend retreat for Dubai residents. The clear, warm waters around nearby **Snoopy Island** are particularly popular with scuba divers.

On the beach at Al Aqah

WHAT TO DO

Adecade of energetic tourism development has provided Dubai with attractions for all tastes. You can watch international entertainers and sporting champions perform, shop till you drop in the souks or air-conditioned malls, play on championship golf courses, or even ski on indoor slopes.

ORGANISED TOURS

Desert trip. Most 4x4 tours depart in the morning or late afternoon. Later tours are usually combined with a dune dinner and entertainment (belly dancing and henna body painting) after sunset at the tour company's torch-lit *bedu*-style desert camp *(see pages 119–20)*.

Dhow cruise. A traditional way of experiencing Dubai Creek is by *dhow*. Daily guided tours and/or lunch and dinner cruises are run by Tour Dubai/Creekside Leisure (tel: 04 336 8407), Creek Cruises (tel: 04 393 9860) and the Radisson SAS (tel: 04 205 7333), all on the Deira waterfront; and, on the Bur Dubai side of the creek, by Al Boom Tourist Village near Garhoud Bridge (tel: 04 324 3000) and Danat Dubai Cruises on Al Seef Road (tel: 04 351 1117). A more cost-effective and flexible option is to negotiate with an *abra* (water taxi) operator for your own tour of the creek, which should cost no more than Dhs30–50 per half-hour per person.

Air tours. Half-hour city sightseeing flights with Aerogulf Services (tel: 04 220 0331) cost around Dhs3,000 for up to four passengers. Alternatively, try Heli Dubai (tel: 04 224 4033). The best way to see the desert is by hot-air balloon.

Andre Agassi and Roger Federer playing on the helipad of Burj Al Arab to promote the Dubai Duty Free Men's Open

Balloon Adventures Dubai (tel: 04 285 4949) offers one-hour flights, but set aside five hours for the experience, including the road trip from your hotel.

SPORT

Participant Sports

Golf. Dubai's most famous 18-hole courses are at the Emirates (tel: 04 380 2222) and Dubai Creek (tel: 04 295 6000) clubs. The Emirates' 7,211-yard par 72 Majlis, the venue for the Dubai Desert Classic, was the first grass course in the Middle East, but newer courses such as the par 72 Montgomerie at Emirates Hills (tel: 04 390 5600), designed by Colin Montgomerie, and the par 72 Desert Course at Arabian Ranches (tel: 04 366 3000), designed by Ian Baker-Finch with Nicklaus Design, are fast gaining international reputations. A more recent addition is the par 72 Al Badia at the Four Seasons Golf Club (tel: 04 601 0101), designed by Robert Trent Jones II, at Dubai Festival City.

Tennis. Most of Dubai's resort hotels have good-quality hard courts as part of their fitness centre offerings. Dubai's premier tennis venue is The Aviation Club in Garhoud (tel: 04 282 4122). Courts are available to non-members on an hourly basis for a charge that includes use of the club's other facilities. There are public tennis courts in Safa Park (tel: 04 349 2111).

Watersports. Most resort hotels offer Hobie catamarans, wind-surfing boards and kayaks for guest use. For offshore sailing try Bluesail Dubai (tel: 04 888 0234); Dubai Offshore Sailing Club (tel: 04 394 1669); or Fun Sports (tel: 050 525 1774), which operates out of several beach clubs. The centre for watersports activity on the coast is Dubai International Marine Club (DIMC) in Mina Seyahi (tel: 04 399 5777).

In the desert. Novel sports include sand-skiing and sand-boarding, which visitors can try on organised tours.

Colin Montgomerie's course at Emirates Hills

Skiing. The Middle East's first indoor ski resort, Ski Dubai at Mall of the Emirates (Sun–Wed 10am–11pm, Thur 10am–midnight, Fri 9am–midnight, Sat 9am–11pm), has five ski runs of up to 400 metres on 'real' snow, including the world's first indoor black run, and a Snow Park with bobsled ride and snowball-throwing gallery. The entry pass includes warm clothing, but not hats or gloves. Absolute beginners aren't allowed on the slopes without first taking lessons at the Snow School.

Spectator Sports

Tennis. The two-week US$2 million Dubai Tennis Championships (www.dubaitennischampionships.com), at the Aviation Club in late February/early March, consists of separate, back-to-back women's WTA and men's ATP tournaments and attracts the world's top players. The annual ITF Al Habtoor Tennis Challenge, held at the Habtoor Grand Resort and Spa in Mina Seyahi, attracts the rising stars of the women's game.

Golf. The annual US$2.4 million Dubai Desert Classic (www.dubaidesertclassic.com), a PGA European Tour event, is held at the Emirates club on Sheikh Zayed Road. The four-day tournament, held in February, attracts the biggest names in the sport – Tiger Woods, Ernie Els and Greg Norman to name a few.

Rugby. The Dubai Rugby Sevens (www.dubairugby7s.com), part of the IRB Sevens World Series, has grown to rival the Hong Kong Sevens in terms of the atmosphere around its 22,000-seat main pitch. The three-day event is held in December at new premises on Al Ain Road, past Dubailand.

Horse racing. The racing season at Nad Al Sheba Racecourse (www.dubairacingclub.com) runs between October

The Racing Maktoums

Dubai's ruling family has become synonymous with international horse racing, thanks mostly to the success of the Godolphin stable, established by Sheikh Mohammed and his brother Sheikh Hamdan in 1994 and named after Godolphin Arabian, a horse that was taken from the Yemeni desert to Europe in the early 18th century to become one of the three founding stallions of the modern thoroughbred.

The stable has trained such greats as Lammtarra, Swain, Daylami and Dubai Millennium. Typically, after a winter in Dubai, the Godolphin team heads to Europe, where its horses are stabled for the summer in Newmarket, the English town where Sheikh Mohammed is said to have acquired his love for horse racing in the 1960s while studying in nearby Cambridge. From Newmarket, the horses travel the world, to be ridden by the world's top jockeys competing in the stable's distinctive blue silks.

On top of their Godolphin interests, the Maktoums also have private studs. In 1997, the late Sheikh Maktoum was the most successful owner in Europe, with group wins in five countries.

and April, with up to seven races run under floodlights on Thursdays from 7pm (9pm during Ramadan). From January to March, race nights are held under the banner of the Dubai International Racing Carnival, culminating in the richest race day in the world, the US$21.25 million Dubai World Cup, which is held in late March: www.dubai worldcup.com.

Nad Al Sheba

Camel racing. The 'Sport of Sheikhs' can be watched between October and May at Dubai Camel Racecourse in Nad Al Sheba. Races are run on Thursdays and Fridays and on national holidays.

Showjumping. The world's richest showjumping event, the US$1.25 million Al Maktoum Memorial Challenge (www.al maktoumchallenge.com), an FEI World Cup qualifier event, is held over three days at the Emirates Riding Centre, Nad Al Sheba, in January.

Motorsport. The UAE Desert Challenge (www.uaedesert challenge.com) is an FIA-sanctioned off-road motor rally that covers some 1,904km (1,183 miles) of the desert interior every November. Dubai Autodrome hosts an FIA GT Championship in November, but Formula 1 fans should head to neighbouring Abu Dhabi for its annual F1 Grand Prix.

Water sports. Sailing and rowing races for traditional boats are held off Mina Seyahi and on Dubai Creek several times a year. The Mina Seyahi coast also hosts two rounds of the UIM Class I World Powerboat Championship in November/December.

OUTDOOR PURSUITS

Quad biking. For quad biking in the desert dunes, head for the cluster of small activity centres some 50km (31 miles) from the city on Route 44 to Hatta.

Scuba diving. PADI courses are run by Al Boom Diving on Al Wasl Road (tel: 04 342 2993, www.alboomdiving.com); Pavilion Dive Centre at the Jumeirah Beach Hotel in Umm Suqeim (tel: 04 406 8828); and Scubatec in Karama (tel: 04 334 8988). Scuba Dubai (tel: 04 341 4940), in Al Quoz, off Sheikh Zayed Road, rents out equipment on a 24-hour basis to experienced divers.

Horse riding. Dubai Polo and Equestrian Club (tel: 04 361 8111) at Arabian Ranches offers desert rides and lessons. Club Joumana (tel: 04 883 6000) at Jebel Ali Golf Resort and Spa offers one-hour desert rides for experienced riders in winter, as well as lessons for beginners. Other venues include Emirates Riding Centre (tel: 04 336 1394), in Nad Al Sheba.

SHOPPING

With thriving souks, modern malls and the annual Dubai Shopping Festival (DSF), which starts in January, Dubai is the proverbial shopper's paradise.

Where to Buy

Souks. Dubai's most famous and most frequented souk is the Gold Souk in Deira. Nearby is the Spice Souk, where Omani frankincense and saffron are among the fragrant offerings. Across the creek, Bur Dubai Souk is the place for textiles. Generally, souk opening hours are Sat–Thur 9.30am–1pm and 4–10pm, Fri 4–10pm. Bargaining is expected and shoppers should always ask for the 'best price'. Although it was only completed in 2004, the indoor

Souk Madinat Jumeirah brilliantly recreates an Arabian souk atmosphere on the Jumeira coast.

Malls. In a city where temperatures can reach uncomfortable highs, Dubai's ultra-modern, air-conditioned malls are the equivalent of neighbourhood high streets. Among the largest and best are Mall of the Emirates on Sheikh Zayed Road in Al Barsha, Ibn Battuta Mall in Jebel Ali, Dubai Festival City and BurJuman Centre in Bur Dubai. Older malls such as Al Ghurair City and Deira City Centre are still going strong.

Wafi Mall and Emirates Towers Boulevard are two of the city's more exclusive malls. Some, such as Ibn Battuta, Wafi and Mercato malls on Jumeira Road, are themed (global destinations, Egyptian pyramids and Italy respectively). New malls are springing up fast: some of the largest in the world are in ambitious property developments such as Downtown Burj Dubai, near Interchange No. 1 on Sheikh Zayed Road (The Dubai Mall), and Dubai Marina (Marina Mall). Generally, opening hours are daily 10am–1pm, and until midnight on Thursday, Friday and Saturday, though some are closed Friday mornings, and prices are fixed.

Karama. Dubai's bargain basement, 18b Street in the Karama district, is lined with stores selling clothing and souvenir items at low prices.

Inside Mall of the Emirates

Carpets for sale on the road to Hatta

What to Buy

Gold. The place to go for gold in Dubai is undoubtedly the Gold Souk in Deira, where yellow and rose gold is available in 18, 21, 22 and 24 carats at prices determined by the international daily gold rate – but do bargain for the 'best price'. If you want to see what's on offer elsewhere before you buy, visit the Gold and Diamond Park near Interchange No. 4 on Sheikh Zayed Road.

Carpets. Though there isn't a carpet souk as such, the greatest concentration of Iranian, Afghan and other regional carpet sellers is in Deira Tower in Al Nasr Square, Deira. National Iranian Carpets, which has an outlet there, also has shops in Deira City Centre, Mercato Mall and Souk Madinat Jumeirah. The best buys are to be had at 'Carpet Oasis' during the annual shopping festival in January (check the local press for venue details). The cramped upstairs area of the Blue Souk in Sharjah also has some excellent carpet shops.

Fabrics. Thanks to its long-established links with the Indian subcontinent, Dubai is a great place for high-quality, low-cost fabrics. Bur Dubai Souk has a concentration of textile traders, but nearby Al Fahidi Street also has some very good shops. Pashminas are widely available.

Perfume. Distinctive Arabian scents are available from Ajmal Perfumes at Al Ghurair City, BurJuman Centre, Deira City Centre, Emirates Towers Boulevard and Mall of the Emirates; and Arabian Oud, at Deira City Centre and Wafi Mall.

Souvenirs. A great one-stop shop is the Arabian Treasures section in Deira City Centre. From toy camels to Arabian coffeepots, *shisha* pipes and framed *khanjar* daggers, it's all here and it's OK to bargain. For items crafted by Dubai-based artisans, browse among the stalls at Marina Market, held at Dubai Marina on Fridays from October to April, or the Khan Murjan underground souk at Wafi Mall. Marina Gulf Trading, which has a large warehouse shop in Al Barsha, and outlets in Deira City Centre and Souk Madinat Jumeirah, has ornate doors, furniture and knick-knacks from India.

The Creative Art Centre, near Town Centre Mall on Jumeira Road, is a treasure-trove of artwork, old maps, antique Arabian jewellery and wooden items from the UAE and Oman. Pictures by local or Dubai-based artists can be purchased at galleries such as the Majlis and XVA in Bastakiya and Gallery One/Middle East Arts at Souk Madinat Jumeirah. Dubai-based artist Susan Walpole has various lines featuring her distinctive Arabian scenes, from notebooks to mouse mats and mugs, at her shop in Jumeirah Plaza and a stall at Mall of the Emirates.

DSF

The month-long Dubai Shopping Festival (DSF) was established in 1996. In 2008, it attracted 3.2 million visitors who spent about Dhs10 billion.

ENTERTAINMENT

Nightlife

Dubai has a vibrant bar and nightclub scene. The busiest evenings tend to be on or around the local weekend (Wednesday, Thursday, Friday), though other nights can be just as busy at venues with 'ladies night' promotions. Dubai doesn't have a nightlife district as such: the best venues – most commonly in hotels or attached to sports and leisure facilities – are spread throughout the city.

On the Deira side of Dubai Creek, the **Irish Village** at Dubai Tennis Stadium (daily 11am–1.30am) is one of the city's best-loved watering holes and has a large outdoor seating area in a pleasant leafy setting. In winter, the open-air **QD's** (daily 6pm–2am), beside the creek at Dubai Creek Golf and Yacht Club, is popular both for early-evening sundowners and late-night dancing under the stars.

On the Bur Dubai side of the creek, there are a cluster of excellent venues at Wafi in Umm Hurair, including the vaguely colonial **Carter's** bar (Mon–Wed, Fri–Sat noon–1am, Sun noon–3am, Thur noon–2am) and the Asian cocktail lounge **Ginseng** (Fri–Wed 7pm–2am, Thur 7pm–3am).

Popular bars on Sheikh Zayed Road include the classy **Vu's Bar** (daily 6pm–3am), which offers stunning views of Jumeira from the 51st floor of the Jumeirah Emirates Towers Hotel. Across the road, in the Towers Rotana hotel, is the lively **Long's Bar** (daily noon–2.30am).

On the Jumeira coast, Dubai Marine Beach Resort and Spa has a number of popular bars, including **Sho Cho's** (daily 7pm–3am), an über-cool Japanese bar, lounge and restaurant with indoor and open-air seating. At the Jumeirah Beach Hotel, golf carts transport visitors to **360°** (daily 4pm–2am), a rooftop bar above a seafood restaurant in the hotel marina that offers a fantastic view of Burj Al Arab. On the 27th floor of Burj Al Arab itself is the breathtaking **Skyview Bar** (tel: 04 301 7438; midday–2am; reservations required).

The fabulous Madinat Jumeirah resort has a number of wonderful waterfront venues: at the Mina A'Salam hotel is the **Bahri Bar** (daily noon–2am), which offers stunning balcony views of the resort and the nearby Burj Al Arab; at the Al Qasr hotel is **Koubba** (daily 4pm–2am), a cocktail bar with similar views to the Bahri Bar from its terrace; at Souk Madinat Jumeirah the choice includes **BarZar** (Sat–Thur 5pm–2am, Fri midday–2am), **The Agency** (Sat–Wed 6pm–1am, Thur 6pm–2am, Fri 5pm–1am) and **Trader Vic's** (daily noon–3pm and 6pm–1.30am).

Further along the coast, Le Meridien Mina Seyahi has the open-air beachside **Barasti Bar** (daily 11am–2am), while the Grosvenor House Hotel at Dubai Marina has both the trendy **Buddha Bar** (Sun–Wed 7pm–2am, Thur 7pm–3am) and **Bar 44** (daily 6pm–2am, Thur until 3am), which has a nice view of The Palm Jumeirah.

Dubai has several world-class nightclubs, with guest DJs regularly flown in from Europe and the United States. Among the hippest are the **Apartment Lounge and Club** at Jumeirah Beach Hotel (Tue and Thur–Fri 9pm–3am), and **Peppermint Lounge Club** at locations

Japengo Café ambience

The Ibn Battuta Mall contains a 21-screen megaplex and IMAX

including the Fairmont hotel on Sheikh Zayed Road and the Madinat Arena in Jumeira. Other popular nightclubs include the classical French-styled **Boudoir** (daily 7pm–3am) at Dubai Marine Beach Resort and Spa, and the Moroccan-themed **Kasbar** (Mon–Sat 9.30pm–3am) at the One&Only Royal Mirage.

Cinema

Dubai has a number of modern, multi-screen cinemas attached to shopping malls. The offerings are mainly mainstream Hollywood movies, with few art-house pictures or regionally made films. The city has two IMAX screens, at Ibn Battuta Mall and Zabeel Park, near Trade Centre Roundabout. The showing of free double-bills at open-air venues in winter has become popular – try 'Movies Under The Stars' on the Wafi rooftop on Sundays from 8pm. XVA Gallery in Bastakiya and the Third Line and Jam Jar galleries in Al Quoz, off Sheikh Zayed Road, also screen free arthouse movies. Check local press for the schedules. The highlight of the year is the Dubai International Film Festival, which takes place at Madinat Jumeirah in December and attracts directors, producers and stars from Hollywood, Bollywood and the Middle East.

Live Music

As well as attracting old favourites such as Elton John, Phil Collins and Lionel Ritchie, Dubai dates are becoming more common on the world-tour schedules of contemporary chart toppers such as the Black Eyed Peas and Kylie Minogue. Opera fans delight in occasional visits by its stars, while for jazz fans there's the annual Dubai International Jazz Festival in February. For further information, check the weekly local listings magazine *Time Out Dubai* or the monthly *What's On*. Desert Rock Festival is held at Dubai Festival City every March and features rock and metal acts.

Many bars around town have live music. On Friday evenings in winter, the Wafi rooftop garden, next to the Spanish *tapas* bar Seville's, hosts the open-air **Peanut Butter Jam** sessions (Fri 8pm–midnight), featuring sets by musicians from the various venues around Wafi. Entry is free, and the crowd lounges on multicoloured bean-bags in front of the stage. For jazz, head to **JamBase** (Mon–Sat 7pm–2am) at Souk Madinat Jumeirah; **Up On The 10th** (daily 6pm–2.45am), which overlooks the Deira creekside from the Radission SAS hotel; or the **Blue Bar** (daily 2pm–2am) at the Novotel, off Sheikh Zayed Road.

Performing Arts

Traditional folk dances are performed by local men in parks and plazas during national holidays and festivals. Dubai's first purpose-built theatre at Madinat Jumeirah (tel: 04 366 8888) is large enough to accommodate West End musicals, but aside from one-offs and occasional runs since its opening in 2004, it has been slow to develop a full season of entertainment. Dubai Drama Group has a permanent home in the Dubai Community Theatre and Arts Centre (tel: 04 341 4777) at Mall of the Emirates, which also hosts English-language touring productions. The Laughter Factory has been bringing British comedians to the city for several years. Live song and dance shows by Bollywood stars have become annual events, catering largely to Dubai's huge Indian community. The annual Dubai Shopping Festival in January attracts a number of international acts for children and adults. For the latest information consult *Time Out Dubai* or *What's On* magazines.

DUBAI FOR CHILDREN

Several shopping malls have dedicated entertainment centres, including Deira City Centre (**Magic Planet**), Wafi Mall (**Encounter Zone**), Mall of the Emirates (**Magic Planet**) and Ibn Battuta Mall (**Fun City**). In Umm Hurair, **Children's City** (Sat–Thur 9am–8.30pm, Fri 3–8.30pm; charge), in Creekside Park, is a brightly coloured, interactive learning zone and amusement facility for children aged between five and 12. Nearby, the **WonderLand Theme and Water Park** (opening hours change throughout the year; tel: 04 324 1222/3222 to check; charge) offers various fairground-style rides. On the Jumeira coast, **Wild Wadi Water Park** (Nov–Feb 10am–6pm, Mar–May and Sept–Oct 10am–7pm, June–Aug 10am–8pm; charge) has 30 rides for all the family.

Fun and games for kids

Calendar of Events

January: Dubai Marathon; Dubai International Horse Show, Nad Al Sheba; Traditional Rowing Race, Dubai Creek; Al Ain Aerobatic Show.

January–February: Dubai Shopping Festival, various venues.

January–March: Dubai International Racing Carnival, Nad Al Sheba Racecourse (Thursday evenings).

February: Dubai Desert Classic European PGA Golf Tournament, Emirates Golf Course; Dubai International Jazz Festival, Dubai Media City; Traditional Dhow Race, Mina Seyahi; Dubai Dog Show, Nad Al Sheba.

February–March: Dubai Tennis Championships, men's ATP and women's WTA tournaments, The Aviation Club, Garhoud; Maktoum Offshore Sailing Trophy, Mina Seyahi.

March: Dubai World Cup, the world's richest horse race, Nad Al Sheba Racecourse; Dubai International Arabian Horse Championship and Dubai International Horse Fair; UAE National Sailing Championship, Mina Seyahi; Dubai International Boat Show; Dubai Art Fair.

March/April: President's Cup Regatta; Dubai-Muscat Sailing Race.

May: Ra'as Hussyan Traditional Dhow Sailing Trophy, Mena Seyahi; Maktoum Cup Rowing Race, on Dubai Creek; Arabian Travel Market, Dubai International Exhibition Centre.

June: Traditional Dhow Race, Mina Seyahi.

June–August: Dubai Summer Surprises, the summer shopping festival.

October–April: Horse-racing season at Nad Al Sheba Racecourse (Thursday evenings); camel racing season at Nad Al Sheba (Thursday and Friday mornings).

October/November: UAE Desert Challenge, off-road motor sport; Gulf Information Technology Exhibition and Computer Shopper retail event.

November: FIA GT Championship race, Dubai Autodrome.

November/December: UIM Class I World Powerboat Championship Grand Prix races, Mina Seyahi.

December: UAE National Day (2 December); Dubai Rugby Sevens, Dubai Exiles Club, Ras Al Khor; Dubai International Film Festival, Madinat Jumeirah; ITF Al Habtoor Tennis Challenge, Dubai Marina.

EATING OUT

As an established hub for business, tourism and sport, it's inevitable that cosmopolitan Dubai should also be developing into a regional centre for world-class cuisine. According to British celebrity chef Gordon Ramsay, who opened his first restaurant outside the UK in Dubai in 2001, 'There's no shadow of a doubt that Dubai can become a culinary hub like Paris or London in the next five to 10 years.'

From downtown *shawarma* (kebab) outlets selling delicious Arabic-style spiced chicken or lamb sandwiches for less than Dhs10 to a luxury waterfront restaurant in one of the city's dozens of five-star hotels, diners are faced with a huge variety of venues and cuisines.

Even if you decide on 'Arabic' food, you're still spoilt for choice: Lebanese, Moroccan or Egyptian – what's it going to be? And where? Among the expat Arab families and Emirati youths at a cheap roadside café, or at a luxury resort hotel?

MEAL TIMES

Meals are eaten at the times you'd expect in any international city: breakfast from 6.30 to 9am, lunch between noon and 3pm and dinner not earlier than 8pm. That said, outside of hotels many cafés and restaurants are open from breakfast to the early hours of the next morning.

On Fridays, the local weekend, take advantage of the set price 'all you can eat' brunches offered in a number of hotels and non-hotel venues around town, generally starting between 11am and 12.30pm and ending between 3 and 4pm.

The one time of year when the opening hours of cafés and restaurants vary from the norm is during Ramadan, when Muslims fast during the day for a month. Throughout this period, which moves from year to year, even non-Muslims are forbidden to eat, drink or smoke in public between sunrise and sunset. Accordingly, non-hotel restaurants are closed until sunset, though some may keep their kitchens open to serve take-away meals. During the day, it's possible to eat in hotel restaurants that are shielded from view behind wooden screens, but alcohol won't be served until the evening.

WHERE TO EAT

If you enjoy alcohol with your meal, your options for eating out are immediately restricted to licensed restaurants in hotels and clubs. But while the right to serve alcohol is confined to these venues, excellence certainly isn't, and it would be a mistake to assume that the many unlicensed premises in the city are somehow sub-standard.

Eat alfresco at Kan Zaman on the creek at Shindagha

Dubai has a number of restaurants and home-grown franchises on its streets and in its malls that combine excellent food with a great atmosphere, and it's in such venues that Emiratis and expats mingle.

Hotels

For a truly memorable meal in a remarkable – and very expensive – setting, consider the Al Mahara seafood restaurant in Dubai's only 'seven-star' hotel, the landmark Burj Al Arab. To enhance their anticipation of its underwater themed decor and enormous central aquarium, not to mention the element of theatre that comes with dining in one of the world's most luxurious hotels, guests are 'transported' to the venue in a virtual 'sub-marine'. Alternatively, for those who prefer a bird's-eye view of the Gulf, 200m (656ft) above the sea in Burj Al Arab is the international Al Muntaha ('highest') restaurant.

For more pie in the sky consider Vu's on the 50th floor of Jumeirah Emirates Towers Hotel; or the revolving Al Dawaar buffet restaurant at the Hyatt Regency in Deira. For a combination of good food and an ocean view, head for the fabulous seafood served at Pierchic, at the end of a pier at Al Qasr in the Madinat Jumeirah resort, which has an outstanding view of Burj Al Arab. Then there's the French La Baie and Italian Splendido, which offer Gulf views at the Ritz-Carlton; the international Celebrities amid the Moroccan-inspired architecture of the One&Only Royal Mirage; and the Arabian Café Arabesque, which overlooks Dubai Creek at the Park Hyatt in Deira.

If you're more concerned about the food than the view, consider Gordon Ramsay's

Dining beside Jumeira Mosque at La Marquise, Palm Strip

Verre, a French restaurant at the Hilton Dubai Creek in Deira or Gary Rhodes' Rhodes Mezzanine at the Grosvenor House Hotel. On Sheikh Zayed Road, Spectrum On One at The Fairmont and Teatro at the Towers Rotana are popular

Eating out guides

Dubai's annual eating out guides are *Eating & Drinking* from *Time Out Dubai*, *Eating Out in the Emirates* from *What's On*, and *Posh Nosh, Cheap Eats & Star Bars*, by Explorer Publishing.

restaurants with international menus. For a mixture of French, Spanish and Italian fare in a Mediterranean courtyard setting try Focaccia at the Hyatt Regency in Deira. Arguably the best Lebanese restaurant in town is Al Nafoorah in the boulevard at Jumeirah Emirates Towers Hotel. For a taste of Japan, consider Nobu at Atlantis the Palm or Kiku at Le Meridien Dubai, near the airport. Just around the corner, the Al Bustan Rotana houses Benihana and a great Thai restaurant, Blue Elephant, though the nearby Le Meridien competes with Sukhothai. For steaks, few venues rival JW's at the JW Marriott in Deira, which also has the international Market Place, where there's a fixed-price 'all you can eat and drink promotion' every night.

In general, dress up for hotels – collared shirts for men, jackets for swanky venues – and make a reservation.

Clubs

The Boardwalk, overlooking the marina and creek at Dubai Creek Golf and Yacht Club, is a perennially popular venue for dining under the stars from an international menu. Nearby, the Aviation Club in Garhoud has the international Cellar and Century Village, a cluster of restaurants that includes the popular Lebanese Mazaj. Across the creek, Pyramids at Wafi is home to the Spanish *tapas* bar Seville's; and Asha's, an Indian restaurant owned by the superstar Bollywood playback singer Asha ('Brimful of Asha') Bhosle.

On the Street

The streets of Dubai are the place for value-for-money Arabic food. Popular no-frills Lebanese eateries include Automatic on Sheikh Zayed Road (also at Beach Centre, Jumeira, and Al Rigga Road, Deira); Al Safadi, in Al Kawakeb Building A, Sheikh Zayed Road (also on Al Rigga Road); and Beirut, on Al Diyafah Street in Satwa. The Olive House on Sheikh Zayed Road is a chic Beirut-style venue that's popular with expat Lebanese. Al Dahleez at Al Boom Tourist Village and Kan Zaman on the Shindagha creekside are more tourist-oriented, but don't compromise on authenticity and offer hard-to-find Emirati dishes. Bastakiah Nights in Bastakiya offers Arabian and Iranian food in a unique heritage setting near the creek. For Lebanese-style fish, consider Sammach in the Beach Centre, Jumeira.

The streets are where you'll also find delicious cheap curries, particularly in the Karama 'curry corridor' opposite the BurJuman Centre. The legendary Ravi's is opposite the Rydges Plaza Hotel in Satwa. One of the best non-hotel Thai restaurants in town is Lemongrass near Lamcy Plaza in Oud Metha, near Umm Hurair.

Home-grown franchises that sum up lively, cosmopolitan Dubai include the New Zealand-owned Lime Tree Café near Jumeira Mosque (there's another outlet in Ibn Battuta Mall); the Emirati-owned Asian/international Japengo on Sheikh Zayed Road (also consider the original at Palm Strip Mall, Jumeira, and other outlets in Wafi Mall, Ibn Battuta Mall and on the waterfront at Souk Madinat Jumeirah); and the chintzy Shakespeare and Company in the Al Attar Business Tower on Sheikh Zayed Road (also at the Village Mall, Jumeira, and Park 'n' Shop, Al Wasl Road). Other gems include the funky Dutch-owned More in Garhoud; Cosmo and Bocadillo on Sheikh Zayed Road; and the Basta Art Café in Bastakiya.

A chef slices *shawarma* meat at the Global Village

Malls

All malls have food courts offering the usual international fast food and chain restaurants, but look out for appealing venues that are located away from the food courts. At Wafi there's the arty European Elements café and the Lebanese deli and restaurant Wafi Gourmet. At Mercato in Jumeira and the Bur-Juman Centre in Bur Dubai there's the French boulangerie and café Paul. The classy Australian café chain Dôme has outlets at BurJuman, Jumeira Plaza and Souk Madinat Jumeirah. An alternative to the American and European coffee franchises in Jumeira is Gerard in Magrudy's Mall, a Dubai institution. Almaz by Momo, at Mall of the Emirates, is worth a visit for its sumptuous North African cuisine.

Dinner Cruises

Options for dining on traditional wooden *dhows* include the Al Mansour, operated by the Radisson SAS Hotel in Deira,

Dates straight from the palm

and the vessels that sail from Al Boom Tourist Village. Bateaux Dubai, the Dubai arm of the dinner cruise company that plies the Seine in Paris and the Thames in London, has a modern glass-panelled vessel that sails daily from Al Seef Road in Bur Dubai.

WHAT TO EAT

Though it is not widely available, Emirati food consists of simple rice, fish or meat dishes, such as *matchbous* (spiced lamb with rice), *hareis* (slow-cooked wheat and lamb) and *fareed* (a meat and vegetable stew poured over thin bread).

The most commonly found Arabic food is Lebanese. Grilled main courses – such as lamb or chicken *shawarma* sliced from a vertical spit, or mixed grills and locally caught fish – are served with Arabic bread, French fries or rice, and are complemented by hot and cold *mezze*.

Hot *mezze* includes *kebeh*, fried minced lamb with crushed wheat; *sambousek*, *samosa*-style pastries filled with minced lamb and pine nuts or haloumi cheese or spinach; and *arayes*, bread stuffed with minced lamb, tomato and cheese. Cold *mezze* includes *hummus*, a dip made from chickpeas and *tahini* (sesame-seed paste); *moutabbal*, a paste of grilled aubergine with *tahini* and lemon; *tabouleh*, a finely chopped parsley salad with mint, fresh tomatoes, onion and crushed wheat, topped with olive oil and lemon; and *fattoush*, a green salad with toasted bread. Several plates of *mezze* make up a meal.

Arabic desserts include *kashta*, which is clotted cream topped with pistachio, pine nuts and honey; and *Umm Ali* (literally, 'Mother of Ali'), a bread and butter pudding with sultanas and coconut, topped with nuts.

Arabic or Lebanese 'fast food' comprises of sandwiches made with Arabic bread and a variety of fillings, including *shawarma* or *falafel* (mashed chickpeas and spices deep fried in flattened balls), served with a salad garnish. Also worth sampling is *manakeesh*, a round, pizza-like bread covered with *zatar*, a mixture of dried thyme, sesame seed, spices and olive oil.

Though the Muslim population is forbidden to eat pork or consume alcohol, both are used as ingredients on many hotel menus and are flagged up for those who must abstain. Without exception, all other meat is halal. Non-hotel venues substitute beef bacon and beef or chicken sausages for pork.

Smoke and Water

By no means a healthy pastime, *shisha* smoking is nonetheless a very popular way to round off a meal in many Arabic restaurants. *Shisha* are free-standing water pipes consisting of a water-filled container topped with tobacco, a small bowl of glowing charcoal and a long pipe with mouthpiece. It has been nicknamed 'hubbly-bubbly' in English because of the bubbling sound the water makes as the smoke is drawn through the pipe, but is also known as 'hookah', after *huqqah*, the Arabic word for container, and *nargileh*, which is derived from the Persian for coconut: *nargil* (coconuts were once used to contain the water). Apparently, because the smoke is drawn through water, it is cleansed of much of its nicotine content, but *shisha* can be habit-forming, especially when the tobacco flavours include apple, strawberry, melon, fruit cocktail and cappuccino. If you sample it once or twice for the experience, however, you're unlikely to become hooked on the hookah.

Drinks at the Al Qasr hotel

WHAT TO DRINK

Popular beverages throughout the Gulf are *shai* (tea) and *kahwa* (coffee). Traditional Arabian or Bedouin coffee is flavoured with cardamom and served in little cups without handles. Thick Turkish coffee is commonly served in restaurants. If you don't like it sweet, ask for medium sweet *(wasat)* or without sugar *(bidoon sukkar)*. Tea, also served sweet, commonly comes without milk and is flavoured with cardamom or fresh mint. A fantastic selection of fresh juices is available in Arabic restaurants and at specialist juice stalls.

To Help You Order...

English is widely spoken, so English speakers should not have a problem, particularly in hotels. Arabic-speaking service staff, mostly from the Levant or North Africa, will understand some English, but here are a few Arabic phrases, just in case:

Do you have a table?	**Indaakum towla?**
Is there anyone here who speaks English?	**Haal yoojad ahad yatakaalam al-lugha al-ingleezia?**
May I see the menu, please?	**Laow samaht, ana ureed laeehat ataamm?**
Excuse me.	**Afwan.**
I don't eat meat.	**La akul lahem.**
What do you recommend?	**Maatha tansah?**
May I have the bill, please?	**Fatoura, laow samaht.**
I'd like...	**Ana ureed...**

thank you	**shukran**	I've finished.	**Ana khallast.**
yes	**nam**	no	**la**
beef	**lahem bakar**	milk	**haleeb**
bread	**khobez**	pepper	**bahar**
chicken	**dajaj**	rice	**rouz**
coffee	**kahwa**	salad	**salata**
dessert	**helou**	salt	**melh**
fish	**samak**	sandwich	**sandweesh**
French fries	**batata makleea**	soup	**shorba**
fruit	**fawakah**	tea	**shai**
ice cream	**booza**	vegetables	**khodra**
lamb	**lahem harouf**	water	**mai**

...and Read the Menu

bajella	local variation on boiled *foul*
esh asaraya	cheesecake with cream topping
foul	fava-bean stew with garlic and lemon
ghuzi	whole roast lamb with rice and pine nuts
hallaweeyat	desserts
jarjir	rocket leaves and onion
kofta	minced lamb with parsley and onion
lahem	meat (not including chicken)
logaimat	fried balls made from egg, flour and saffron
mashawee	grills
mehalabiya	milk custard with pistachios and rosewater
nakhi	boiled chick peas
roub	cucumber with yoghurt
salatat zatar	thyme salad with onions, lemon and olive oil
shish kebab	grilled mutton marinated with cumin and cinnamon
shish tawouq	grilled chicken pieces marinated with cumin and cinnamon
toum	crushed garlic and mayonnaise

HANDY TRAVEL TIPS

An A–Z Summary of Practical Information

A

ACCOMMODATION (See also CAMPING, YOUTH HOSTELS and RECOMMENDED HOTELS on page 129)

While one-, two- and three-star accommodation can be found among Dubai's 400-plus hotels and hotel apartments, the vast majority of visitors opt to stay in four- or five-star hotels. It's worth shopping around for the best value: the price for two people sharing a five-star standard de-luxe room ranges from Dhs1,280 per room per night inclusive of tax at the Metropolitan Palace in downtown Deira to Dhs2,960 plus 20 percent tax and service charge at Al Qasr in the Madinat Jumeirah resort (high season). Among the better-value four-star hotels is the Ibis World Trade Centre, which charges Dhs775 per standard de-luxe room, inclusive of tax and service charge, for two people sharing. To avoid Dubai's comparatively high room rates, some visitors stay in neighbouring Sharjah, where prices are generally lower.

Dubai's high-season rates peak in December and April. The low season stretches through the hotter months of June, July and August. Unusually for an international destination, the rates for Dubai's coastal resort hotels are higher than its city-centre hotels, but overall prices are on the up. Room rates also tend to increase whenever a large conference or exhibition is taking place in Dubai. Seasonal promotions and packages with airlines or tour companies, booked from your home country, can result in significant savings on published rack rates.

AIRPORT

Dubai International Airport, otherwise known as DXB (tel: 04 216 2525; www.dubaiairport.com), is centrally located on the Deira side of Dubai Creek, between the Al Garhoud and Al Qusais districts. Its futuristic air traffic control tower and Sheikh Rashid Terminal (Terminal 1), which opened in 2000, are Dubai landmarks in themselves. The new, state-of-the-art Terminal 3, part of a US$4 billion expansion programme, opened in 2008. The new structure accommodates Emirates airline's new A380 'super-jumbos' and has boosted the airport's handling capacity to 60 million passengers per year.

The airport tends to be at its busiest throughout the night. On arrival, to speed you past the long queues at passport control, consider booking the Marhaba ('Welcome') greeting service at least 24 hours in advance (tel: 04 224 5780; www.marhabaservices.com). The charge is Dhs80 per passenger from immigration. As the walk between the terminal and passport control is a long one, electric carts are provided for the elderly and travellers with disabilities. Various kiosks for tourist information, hotels, car rental agencies and money exchanges are beyond the baggage reclaim area. Dubai Transport taxis are off to the left as you exit the airport building.

ALCOHOL

Dubai has a relatively liberal attitude to the consumption of alcohol by non-Muslims as long as it is limited to licensed premises and people don't drink and drive. The emirate is not 'dry' and beers, wines and spirits are readily available in hotels (rooms, restaurants and bars) and clubs, but not, generally, in 'outside' restaurants. Alcohol is not sold in supermarkets and only residents with government-issued liquor licences can buy from licensed vendors MMI and A&E.

Dubai has a zero-tolerance approach to drink-driving and offenders face a lengthy legal process, three weeks in prison and even deportation, whatever the amount of alcohol detected in the blood. It is also an offence to buy alcohol for a Muslim. The sale of alcohol everywhere is restricted during the Islamic holy month of Ramadan.

Finally, visitors should remember that the effects of alcohol are exacerbated by heat and humidity. To avoid dehydration, make sure you drink plenty of water.

B

BOOKSHOPS

Dubai has a number of good English-language booksellers. Among them are Magrudy's (tel: 04 344 4009), which has outlets in Magrudy's Mall in Jumeira, Deira City Centre, Festival City, Ibn Battuta Mall, BurJuman Centre and various Spinney's supermarkets; Jashanmal Bookstores (tel: 04 341 9757) in Mall of the Emirates, The Village Mall in Jumeira, and Wafi Mall; Books Plus (tel: 04 368 5375) in Ibn Battuta Mall, Dubai Marina and various other locations; Borders in Mall of the Emirates (tel: 04 341 5758) and Deira City Centre (tel: 04 295 1010); and Book World by Kinokuniya in The Dubai Mall (04 434 0111). For secondhand books, or to sell on your airport fiction, visit House of Prose in Jumeirah Plaza or Ibn Battuta Mall.

BUDGETING FOR YOUR TRIP

Dubai can be an expensive city to visit and if you don't shop around for the best deal in your choice of airline and hotel, or keep a tight rein on your daily expenditure at restaurants and shopping malls, you'll quickly discover that in common with other Gulf states, it can be very good at parting you from your cash.

Travelling to Dubai. Many find combination airfare-hotel deals cheaper than separately arranged air travel and accommodation. The best prices are low season (July–Sept), but that's the hottest time of the year in the UAE. As a rough guide, packages from the UK, based on two adults and including economy-class airfare and five nights in a deluxe room at a five-star hotel, with airport transfers and breakfast, range from £1,500 in the low season (northern hemisphere summer) to £1,800 in the high-season month of December.

Accommodation. If you're not on a package deal, the cost for a standard double room ranges from around Dhs300–350 per night in a one-star city-centre hotel to Dhs775–1,000 at a four-star hotel, and

Dhs1,000–3,500 at a five-star hotel. A suite at the seven-star Burj Al Arab costs Dhs7,500 per night plus 20 percent tax and service charge.

Meals and drinks. It's possible to eat for as little as Dhs15 per person if you go for a filling sandwich in a street-side Lebanese restaurant or a curry in a no-nonsense Indian or Pakistani outlet. Main courses in most decent Western-style, non-hotel restaurants are Dhs25–40. For fine dining, budget for upwards of Dhs60 per person for main courses. Cans of soft drinks start at Dhs1 in shops, but are marked up by as much as 800 percent in restaurants. Freshly made juices cost Dhs6–15. A tall caffè latte at Starbucks costs Dhs13. Imported alcoholic drinks are generally more expensive than they would be in the West.

Local transport. If you take a Dubai Transport taxi from Dubai International Airport, the metre starts at Dhs25, but it is set at Dhs3.30 elsewhere in the city. The fare from the airport to destinations in Deira and Bur Dubai will be around Dhs30–40, but will be considerably more (Dhs80+) to the more distant resort hotels along the Jumeira coast: if that's where you're staying, take advantage of your hotel's airport transfer service. The ordinary fare for taxis between the resort hotels and the city centre will also be around Dhs80 one way, so consider taking shuttle buses provided by most hotels.

Buses are seldom used by visitors, but bus tickets offer the best value, costing between Dhs1 and Dhs3. A creek crossing on an *abra* (water taxi) is Dhs1. A half-day desert safari with a tour company costs Dhs270 in the low season (northern hemisphere summer) and Dhs310 in the high season. The price of petrol is around Dhs6 per imperial gallon for unleaded Special (95 octane).

BUSINESS HOURS/PUBLIC HOLIDAYS

While Thursday afternoon and Friday is the weekend in the Islamic world, the local weekend in Dubai is Fri–Sat. Friday equates to a Sunday in the West. Banks and many private companies keep business hours on Saturdays.

Generally, government ministries and departments are open Sun–Thur 7.30am–2.30pm; closed Fri–Sat. Most embassies and consulates open Sun–Thur 7.30am–2.30pm, and close Fri and Sat.

Many private-sector companies now follow the Western working day of 9am–6pm, though some offices stick to the traditional split shift with an extended lunch break between 1 and 4pm; these start earlier at 8am and close later at 7pm. During Ramadan, fasting Muslims take a shorter working day and some businesses change their hours accordingly.

The UAE's fixed annual holidays are Accession Day (6 August), UAE National Day (2 December) and New Year's Day. Other holidays, such as Eid Al Fitr and Eid Al Adha (which are linked to the holy month of Ramadan and move forward 11 days each year), the Islamic New Year, Lailat Al Mi'Raj and the Prophet Mohammed's Birthday are determined by the moon and are announced in the local press about a week before.

C

CAMPING

The UAE doesn't have any official campsites, but that doesn't stop local and expat residents camping in the desert dunes on weekends and national holidays. But the best and safest way for visitors to overnight in the desert is with a specialist tour company. Camping on Dubai's public beaches is not allowed without a permit from Dubai Municipality (tel: 04 221 5555).

CAR HIRE (See also Driving)

Hiring a car is one of the best ways to explore the city and emirate of Dubai. Car-hire companies include **Avis** (tel: 04 295 7121), **Hertz** (tel: 04 206 0206), **Budget** (tel: 04 295 6667), **Thrifty** (tel: 800 4694) and **National** (tel: 04 283 2020), most of which have kiosks in the arrivals area of Dubai airport as well as city offices, including all major shopping malls. The daily rate for a mid-size saloon varies between Dhs180 and Dhs366, including insurance and unlimited mileage.

Most national driving licences are recognised, but it's a good idea to have a valid international driving licence with you as back-up in case the rules change. For insurance reasons, visitors can only drive rental cars and not privately owned vehicles. To drive a resident friend's car, for example, visitors must get a temporary licence from Dubai Police.

CLIMATE

Dubai is an arid, desert nation with mild, pleasant winters and very hot, humid summers. While the marketing spin about the country's climate says it enjoys year-round sunshine, the reality is that you can't be out in the sun for long periods in the summer. Unusually for a northern hemisphere destination, summertime is when people spend more time indoors – kept cool by air-conditioning. The period June to September is particularly hot, with temperatures topping 48°C (118°F) during the day, and around 90 percent humidity.

From October to May, however, the weather is glorious, with monthly averages between 22°C (71°F) and 32°C (90°F), and lows of 10°C (50°F): evenings can be quite chilly. Humidity also falls considerably. Weather-wise, this is undoubtedly the best time to visit, but commensurate with the fall in temperatures is a rise in accommodation costs. What rain there is (127mm/5ins fell in 2008) tends to fall on isolated days between October and March, when heavy morning fog can also occur.

CLOTHING

While swimming trunks and bikinis are fine at the beach, it's not acceptable to expose the body in other public areas, such as residential neighbourhoods near beaches, or in souks and malls. Revealing too much skin could cause offence – and that goes as much for men baring their torsos as it does for women revealing too much of theirs (going topless is not an option). It's fine to expose arms and legs, and it's increasingly acceptable for women to bare their shoulders, but shorts and skirts shouldn't ride too high. Generally, men and women are expected to dress modestly, particularly during the Muslim holy month of Ramadan.

Practically, consider that Dubai is hot in summer and warm in winter, so lightweight cottons and linens are advisable. Winter evenings can be surprisingly cool, however, so it will be necessary to pack a cardigan or jumper, particularly if you want to enjoy an alfresco evening meal or if you intend going to an open-air event in the evening.

CRIME AND SAFETY (See also POLICE)

Crime is relatively rare in Dubai. Generally, visitors won't encounter criminal activity and needn't be concerned about being extra cautious with their possessions. Most people feel safe on the city streets even late at night. Certainly, there are no neighbourhoods to avoid or gangs of rabble-rousing youths to steer clear of. That said, rather than drop your guard, it would be wise to maintain the usual precautions you are in the habit of taking elsewhere in the world, and make sure you get comprehensive travel and medical insurance before travelling.

The US-led 'war on terror' has led to increased concerns for the safety of citizens of countries associated with American military activity in the region. The UAE is no exception and vigilance against terrorism is recommended. However, the country is an ally of the United States and ordinary Emiratis are generally friendly to Westerners.

Call Dubai Police's Department for **Tourist Security** on 800 4438.

CUSTOMS AND ENTRY REQUIREMENTS

Visas are available on arrival at Dubai International Airport for business and leisure travellers from 33 countries, including the UK, Ireland, the United States, Canada, Australia, New Zealand, most of Europe and selected Asian nations. The visa is valid for 60 days and can be renewed for a further 30 days at the Department of Naturalisation and Residency (tel: 04 398 0000) near Trade Centre Roundabout, for a renewal charge of Dhs500. Those who don't qualify for a visa on arrival, including South African citizens, can get a 30-day, non-renewable tourist visa through a hotel or tour operator sponsor. This should be arranged before entry to the UAE: visitors should ensure they have a fax copy of the visa with them and they should stop to collect the original at a designated desk in the airport before they head for passport control. The total cost is Dhs110. Nationals of Israel cannot enter the UAE.

The duty-free allowance for arrivals in Dubai is four litres of spirits or wine, 400 cigarettes or 2kg of tobacco, and cigars to the value of Dhs3,000. There's a small duty-free outlet in the arrivals hall.

D

DRIVING (See also CAR HIRE)

Driving is on the right-hand side of the road in Dubai (and in the rest of the UAE), so vehicles are left-hand drive. The speed limits on most city streets are 60–80kph (37–50mph), and 100–120kph (62–75mph) on main highways. On road signs, distances are indicated in kilometres.

The road system in the UAE is good, but the general standard of driving is not: it is generally characterised by aggression, impatience and carelessness. Accordingly, accidents are a common sight and the UAE has one of the highest traffic-accident death rates in the world. Lane discipline is not great, so on roads with more than a single lane in one direction, drivers should be aware of what's happening behind and on either side of them before manoeuvring. Often on main highways, such as Sheikh Zayed Road, aggressive drivers will close in at illegally high speeds on the vehicle in front, flashing it to pull out of their way, regardless of the traffic situation to its right. The fact that major arteries are under radar surveillance seems not to deter high-speed driving. Also bear in mind that around the city, taxi drivers have a nasty habit of swerving, stopping suddenly and blocking traffic if they spot a fare at the roadside, so keep a safe distance behind them – and if you're hailing a cab, please don't encourage such stupidity.

Outside Dubai, particularly on the Hatta highway, there's a possibility of camels wandering onto roads, so be cautious on desert roads, particularly at night on sections that aren't well lit.

The wearing of seat belts is compulsory for drivers and front-seat passengers in the UAE, and children under 10 are not allowed to sit in the front passenger seat.

In the city, it is necessary to pay for parking in designated paid parking zones – look out for the orange signs and solar-powered meters. The cost is Dhs1–2 per hour, depending on the area. The fine for not displaying a valid ticket on the dashboard starts at Dhs100. Speeding fines are Dhs200. Sheikh Zayed Road between Garhoud Bridge and Interchange 4 is a toll road, as is Maktoum Bridge. For details of other traffic violations and fines, visit the Dubai Police website: www.dubaipolice.gov.ae. If you are involved in a road accident, stop and wait for the police. A police report on every level of accident is required for insurance claims. If you are stopped by the police at any time, you must be able to produce your driving licence and car hire/insurance papers (originals, not copies) there and then.

Unless you are an experienced off-road driver, you should not consider hiring a four-wheel drive to head into the desert outside Dubai. The desert is one of the harshest environments known to man and there's a particular technique to driving in it.

E

ELECTRICITY

The mains electricity in Dubai is 220/240 volts and 50 cycles. Wall sockets are designed for British-type, 13-amp three-pin plugs. Adaptors for two-pin appliances are available in supermarkets.

EMBASSIES AND CONSULATES

As Abu Dhabi, not Dubai, is the federal capital of the UAE, Dubai tends to have foreign consulates rather than embassies. The telephone numbers for selected countries are:

Australia: 04 508 7100
Canada: 04 314 5555
Ireland: +966 1 488 2300 (Riyadh, Kingdom of Saudi Arabia)
New Zealand: 04 332 7031
South Africa: 04 397 5222
United Kingdom: 04 309 4444
United States: 04 311 6000

EMERGENCIES (See also POLICE)

Dial 999 for police or ambulance, or 997 for fire.

G

GETTING THERE

Most visitors arrive at Dubai International Airport, though cruise ships dock occasionally at Dubai Cruise Terminal in Port Rashid. Alternatively, some may choose to fly into the neighbouring emirates of Abu Dhabi and Sharjah and cross into Dubai by road. The journey from Abu Dhabi takes between an hour and an hour and a half. Sharjah is closer, but in rush-hour traffic the journey can take an hour.

Dubai's airport, a Middle East hub for international air travel, is the home of the airline Emirates (tel: 04 214 4444; www.emirates. com), which connects Dubai with 84 cities in 55 countries, including destinations in Europe, the US (New York three times daily), South America, Africa, the Far East, Australia and New Zealand.

Thanks to Dubai's open-skies policy, some 105 airlines link Dubai with 147 destinations around the world. Dubai-bound international carriers include: Air France (tel: 0871 66 33 777; www.airfrance. co.uk); British Airways (tel: 0844 493 0787; www.ba.com); Cathay

Pacific (tel: 020 8834 8888; www.cathaypacific.com); Lufthansa (tel: 0871 945 9747; www.lufthansa.com); Royal Brunei (tel: 04 351 4111; www.bruneiair.com); Singapore Airlines (tel: 0844 800 2380; www.singaporeair.com); and Virgin Atlantic (tel: 0870 380 2007; www.virgin-atlantic.com).

America's United Airlines has an office in Dubai (tel: 04 316 6942), but its passengers from the US are routed via London on Emirates or Frankfurt on Lufthansa. Qantas is another offline carrier with a Dubai office (tel: 04 316 6652): its passengers are routed through Singapore on Emirates, or on other Middle East carriers.

The flying time from London to Dubai, direct, is about seven hours.

GUIDES AND TOURS (See also Tourist Information)

Half-day **city sightseeing** tours organised by Dubai's various tour companies combine the main heritage sights with the city's striking modern architecture. An alternative is a hop-on hop-off ticket with the **Big Bus Company** (tel: 04 340 7709), which operates open-top, double-decker buses daily on city and beach routes. To view Dubai from both the highway and the creek, take the amphibious Wonder Bus, operated by **Wonder Bus Tours** (tel: 04 359 5656), which departs three times daily from the BurJuman Centre in Bur Dubai.

From October to April, Arabian Adventures (tel: 04 303 4888) runs half-day **afternoon walks** through the creekside heritage areas in Bur Dubai and Deira. The Sheikh Mohammed Centre for Cultural Understanding (tel: 04 353 6666) runs **walking tours** of historic Bastakiya at 10am on Sundays and Thursdays, and tours of Jumeira Mosque on Saturdays, Sundays, Tuesdays and Thursdays, beginning at 10am. The centre also organises visits to the homes of Emirati families.

The leading tour companies offering **desert safaris** and 'wadi-bashing' trips along dry river beds are Arabian Adventures (tel: 04 303 4888; www.arabian-adventures.com); Desert Rangers (tel: 04 340 2408; www.desertrangers.com); Net Tours (tel: 04 266 6655; www.nettoursdubai.com); Orient Tours (tel: 04 282 8238;

www.orient-tours-uae.com); and Voyagers Xtreme (tel: 04 345 4504, www.turnertraveldubai.com).

The **Breakfast Stable Tour** at Nad Al Sheba Racecourse, organised by the Nad Al Sheba Club (tel: 04 336 3666) offers a rare look at thoroughbreds during their early-morning gallops, as well as a behind-the-scenes tour of the stables and grandstand facilities.

Several licensed operators run half- or full-day big-game **fishing expeditions** into the Arabian Gulf for sailfish, barracuda, kingfish and tuna. These include Bounty Charters (tel: 050 552 6067); Dubai Voyager (tel: 050 886 6227); and Le Meridien Mina Seyahi (tel: 04 399 3333). Fishing equipment is provided and novices are catered for.

For details of *dhow* tours and trips by helicopter or hot-air balloon, see *What To Do, pages 83–4.*

H

HEALTH AND MEDICAL CARE

The main emergency hospital in Dubai is the government-run Rashid Hospital (tel: 04 219 2000) near Maktoum Bridge in Bur Dubai, where treatment is free for emergencies. A consultation with a doctor in cases that are not emergencies costs Dhs100. Alternatively, the government-affiliated Iranian Hospital (tel: 04 344 0250) on Al Wasl Road charges Dhs50 per consultation. For emergencies with children, Al Wasl Hospital (tel: 04 219 3000), across the highway from Wafi, is a renowned paediatric hospital. The number to dial for an ambulance is 999.

L

LANGUAGE

Arabic is the official language in the UAE, but English is widely spoken. It is unlikely that you will encounter any difficulty using English in hotels, restaurants and shopping malls, as many of the staff aren't Arabic-speakers themselves. That said, wherever you meet someone you know is an Arabic-speaker, it would be polite to have a few words and phrases committed to memory.

hello	marhaba
welcome	ahlan wa-sahlan (ahlan)
peace be with you (greeting)	as-salaam alaykum
and with you be peace (response)	wa-alaykum as-salaam
good morning	sabah al khayr
good morning (response)	sabah al nour
good evening	masaa al khayr
good evening (response)	masaa al nour
My name is…	ana ismi…
What is your name?	shou ismac?
How are you?	kayf haalak?
well	zein
you're welcome	afwan
please	min fadlak
thank you	shukran
yes/no	naam/la
finished (as in I have… or it is…)	khallas
goodbye, peace be with you	maa as-salaama

MAPS

Dubai is changing so rapidly that maps of the city quickly become out of date. Among the best is Dubai Municipality's Dubai Tourist Map, which is widely available in the city's hotel shops and book stores. GEOprojects produces a 1:750,000 scale map of the UAE with city maps of central Dubai and other key cities in its Arab World Map Library series. Zodiac Publishing's Satellite Road Map of the United Arab Emirates is a good UAE map.

MEDIA

Dubai's two long-established English-language daily newspapers, *Gulf News* and *Khaleej Times*, face stiff competition from the newer tabloid-size publication *7Days* and the Abu Dhabi-produced *National*, which have rejuvenated investigative reporting in the UAE. The letters page of the free *7Days* is particularly lively and provides a fascinating insight into the minds of the city's residents – both expatriate and local. There are a number of very good magazines published locally, including the events and listings magazines *What's On* and *TimeOut Dubai*, and the business titles *Gulf Business* and *Arabian Business*. Foreign newspapers and English-language publications such as the *International Herald Tribune* and *Weekly Telegraph* can be found in supermarkets.

For English-language talk radio, tune to Dubai Eye on 103.8 FM. Its programming covers current affairs, sport and lifestyle. Music stations broadcasting in English include Dubai 92 (92 FM), Channel 4 (104.8 FM), Emirates Radio 1 (99.3 FM and 100.5 FM) and Emirates Radio 2 (90.5 FM and 98.5 FM).

Local television isn't so good. Dubai One TV offers mostly Western movies and shows, but the local news in English at 8.30pm daily may be of interest. Satellite and cable TV with international news channels such as CNN, BBC World and Sky News is available in hotels.

MONEY

The currency in Dubai is the UAE dirham (Dhs or AED), which is pegged to the US dollar at the rate of Dhs3.675 to US$1. There are 100 fils in a dirham. The notes in circulation are Dhs 5, 10, 20, 50, 100, 200, 500 and 1,000. Be warned that the brown Dhs1,000 note looks a lot like Dhs200. Generally, it's good to carry Dhs100 notes and lower values for day-to-day transactions. The most common coins are the silver Dhs1, 50 fils and 25 fils.

Banks are generally open Sat–Thur 8am–1pm, closed Fri. The best places to change foreign currency and traveller's cheques into dirhams, however, are the numerous exchanges found in malls and souks, which keep shop hours. Among them are Al Ansari Exchange (tel: 04 397 7787), Al Fardan Exchange (tel: 04 228 0004), and Thomas Cook Al Rostamani (tel: 04 332 7444). Hotels may exchange cash and traveller's cheques at non-competitive rates for guests.

Major international credit and debit cards are accepted in large shops, restaurants and hotels. When shopping in souks, it's better to bargain for the 'best price' with cash.

P

PHOTOGRAPHY

Visitors should ask permission before taking photos of Emiratis in national dress. Generally, Emirati women do not like having their picture taken, even when covered. The best place to photograph local men and women is the Heritage and Diving Village in Dubai or at Hatta Heritage Village, where they are used to the attention. Photography is not allowed at Dubai International Airport or military bases.

POLICE (See also CRIME AND SAFETY)

Dubai's police force has a low-key but visible presence in the emirate – its green and white BMW and Mercedes patrol cars are a common sight on the main highways and in residential neighbourhoods. During rush hour, the traffic flow at busy intersections is often managed by police motorcyclists. The emergency number for the police is 999. The toll-free number for general information, including details about the force's Department for Tourist Security, is 800 4438. The police website is www.dubaipolice.gov.ae.

POST OFFICES

Dubai's Central Post Office (Sat–Thur 8am–8pm, Fri 5–9pm) is located on Zabeel Road in Karama. There are smaller post offices scattered around the city, including Deira (near the Avari Hotel), Satwa (near

Ravi's restaurant), Jumeira (on Al Wasl Road) and at Dubai airport. The cost of sending an airmail letter to Western countries is around Dhs3–6 and a postcard around Dhs1–2. Allow 10 days for delivery. International courier companies operating in Dubai include DHL (tel: 800 4004), FedEx (tel: 800 4050) and UPS (tel: 800 4774).

PUBLIC TRANSPORT

For visitors, the most practical forms of transport are Dubai's ubiquitous metered taxis, which can be flagged down on the street or pre-booked. The main companies are Dubai Transport Corporation (tel: 04 208 0808), Metro Taxi (tel: 04 267 3222), National Taxis (tel: 04 339 0002) and Arabia Taxi (tel: 04 285 5566). The cabs are air-conditioned, clean and comfortable.

Dubai's bus service, operated by Dubai Municipality Transport, has yet to win the confidence of the city's Western expatriate population – waiting at bus stops on a hot day is not the most comfortable way to get around town, though air-conditioned bus stops are being introduced. On the creek *abras*, or water taxis, ferry passengers between Bur Dubai and Deira. The new, air-conditioned Waterbus operates from the various creekside water taxi stations in Deira and Bur Dubai. Journeys on the dedicated tourist route, which operates 8am–midnight, cost Dhs25 per person. The Dubai Metro light-rail project, similar to Singapore's MRT and the San Francisco area BART, is being phased in and should do much to alleviate the pressure on the city's increasingly traffic-clogged streets.

R

RELIGION

Islam is the official religion of the UAE, but there is freedom of worship for Christians in church compounds on the understanding that they do not proselytise. Christian churches are grouped along Oud Metha Road in Bur Dubai and in Jebel Ali Village. They include

Dubai Evangelical Church Centre (tel: 04 884 6630), the Anglican Holy Trinity (tel: 04 337 0247) and the Roman Catholic St Mary's (tel: 04 337 0087). The main services are held on Friday – the local weekend. Bibles for personal use can be carried into the country.

S

SMOKING

In 2005, the UAE ratified the World Health Organisation Framework Convention on Tobacco Control, under which it must adhere to international standards on tobacco control measures, such as reducing exposure to passive smoking in public places. Smoking is banned in malls and air-conditioned public spaces, including restaurants, though some restaurants have dedicated smoking zones. In general, the attitude to smoking is similar to that in Western nations. During Ramadan, smoking in public is forbidden during daylight hours.

T

TELEPHONE

The international dialling code for the UAE is 00 971. The code for Dubai landlines is 04 – overseas callers should drop the 0. Calls within Dubai are free. The code for UAE mobile phones is 050 or 055 – again, overseas callers should drop the first 0.

The local telecoms provider, Etisalat (tel: 101 or 144), provides international direct dialling to 170 countries. The code for dialling internationally is 00. Well-maintained Etisalat payphones (card- or coin-operated) are prominently located in public areas and can be found in malls, usually near the prayer room or toilet area. It is possible to call internationally on these public phones. Pre-paid phone cards, which cost Dhs25 or Dhs40, are available from Etisalat, shops, supermarkets and service stations. Roaming mobile users will gain access to the local GSM service. The number for directory enquiries is 181, where assistance is provided in English as well as Arabic. Automated answering systems in Dubai tend to begin in Arabic, so hold on for instructions in English.

TIME DIFFERENCES

Dubai is four hours ahead of GMT/Universal Coordinated Time (UCT), throughout the year. These are the time differences during the northern hemisphere winter:

New York	London	**Dubai**	Jo'burg	Sydney	Auckland
3am	8am	**noon**	10am	7pm	9pm

TIPPING

Tipping is appreciated, but not expected – 10 percent of the bill is acceptable when a service charge has not been added. Service charges are often added automatically in hotel restaurants.

TOILETS

Western-style toilets are commonly found in hotels and restaurants. In malls and other public gathering places there's usually a combination of Western-style and squat toilets.

TOURIST INFORMATION (See also GUIDES AND TOURS)

The Government of Dubai Department of Tourism and Commerce Marketing (DTCM; tel: 04 223 0000; www.dubaitourism.ae) is the emirate's official tourism promotion organisation. DTCM's information centres in Dubai include a kiosk at Dubai International Airport's arrivals hall, and desks in the following malls: Deira City Centre, BurJuman Centre, Wafi, Mercato and Ibn Battuta. There's also an office in Baniyas Square, Deira. The head office is on the 13th floor of the National Bank of Dubai building on the Deira Creekside. DTCM's overseas offices include:

UK & Ireland: Suites 201–206, 1 Northumberland Avenue, London, WC2N 5BW; tel: +44 207 321 6110; e-mail: dtcm_uk@dubaitourism.ae.

North America: 25 West 45th Street, Suite #405, New York, NY, 10036; tel: +1 212 575 2262; e-mail: dtcm_usa@dubaitourism.ae.

Australia & New Zealand: Suite 104, 25–29 Berry Street, North Sydney, NSW 2060; tel: +61 2 9956 6620; e-mail: dtcm_aus@dubaitourism.ae.

South Africa: PO Box 698, 1 Orchard Lane, Rivonia 2128, Johannesburg; tel: +27 11 785 4600; e-mail: dtcm_sa@dubaitourism.ae.

TRAVELLERS WITH DISABILITIES

DTCM *(see above)* publishes a special guide, *Dubai Simply Accessible*, for travellers with disabilities. Among the areas covered are facilities at Dubai International Airport; specialist taxi transport (Dubai Transport; tel: 04 224 5331); access to hotels, heritage sites (including Dubai Museum); desert tours (North Tours; tel: 04 222 2808); cinemas, parks and malls; specialised equipment suppliers; and specialist medical facilities.

Parking provision for people with disabilities is on a par with that in many Western cities. Most hotels have ramps allowing wheelchair access. In modern malls there's usually an elevator (lift) alternative to an escalator. Most toilets in the UAE have enlarged cubicles for wheelchair access.

W

WEBSITES AND INTERNET CAFÉS

The following websites are useful sources of information:
www.7days.ae 7Days
www.ameinfo.com AME Info
www.business24-7.ae Emirates Business 24/7
www.dm.gov.ae Dubai Municipality

www.dubaiairport.com Dubai International Airport
www.dubaidutyfree.com Dubai Duty Free
www.dubaitourism.ae Government of Dubai Department of
   Tourism and Commerce Marketing
www.emirates.com Emirates (airline)
www.gulfnews.com Gulf News
www.princesshaya.net Princess Haya Bint Al Hussein
www.sheikhmohammed.co.ae Sheikh Mohammed Bin Rashid
   Al Maktoum
www.timeoutdubai.com TimeOut Dubai
www.uaeinteract.com UAE Ministry of Information and Culture
   The Etisalat subsidiary Emirates Internet & Media is the main
provider of internet services through the UAE proxy server. Access
to certain websites may be blocked. Internet connection is available
in the guest rooms and business centres of larger hotels. Elsewhere,
internet cafés can be found at various locations; the charges are
around Dhs15–20 per hour. There are also an increasing number of
hot spots offering free wireless connection for laptop users. These
include Coffee Bean & Tea Leaf on Jumeira Road, and French Connection café and Starbucks on Sheikh Zayed Road.

Y

YOUTH HOSTELS

The Dubai Youth Hostel (tel: 04 298 8151), part of the UAE Youth
Hostel Association www.uaeyha.com, is located on Al Nahda Road
on the Al Ghusais side of Dubai International Airport. Stays are limited to a maximum of three days and payment must be made in cash.
Food, alcoholic drinks and smoking are not allowed in the rooms.
   There are also youth hostels in other UAE cities: Sharjah (tel: 06
522 5070) and, on the East Coast, Fujairah (tel: 09 222 2347) and
Khor Fakkan (tel: 09 237 0886). The Dubai hostel's reception is open
24/7. The others are open 8am–midnight. Breakfast is provided.

Recommended Hotels

Dubai has the 'best', 'most luxurious' and one of the tallest hotels in the world, but even if you don't stay at the world-famous Burj Al Arab, luxury awaits you at a growing number of resort and city centre hotels.

The vast majority of the city's tourist and business hotels have a five-star rating, but within the five-star category amenities and prices vary dramatically *(see page 109).*

The accommodation listed below ranges from a youth hostel to one of the world's few 'seven-star' hotels. The price categories indicated by $ symbols next to the hotel name include an additional 20 percent tax and service charge where this is applicable, but if you telephone a hotel yourself, in most cases the figure you'll be quoted won't include this 20 percent. Additionally, in most cases the rate quoted is for room only – breakfast is an additional Dhs75–95.

The price categories below are based on the high-season rate for a standard de-luxe room for two people. They do not indicate star rating. Because so many Dubai hotels are in the five-star category, assume the listing is for a five-star property unless otherwise stated.

$$$$$	Dhs3,500–8,000
$$$$	Dhs2,500–3,500
$$$	Dhs1,000–2,500
$$	Dhs500–1,000
$	Less than Dhs500

DUBAI

JUMEIRA COAST

Al Qasr $$$$$ *Al Sufouh Road, Umm Suqeim, tel: 04 366 8888, fax: 04 366 7788, email: mjinfo@jumeirah.com, www.jumeirah. com.* Its Arabic name means 'The Castle' and this grand boutique hotel really is fit for a king. Part of the Arabian-style Madinat Jumeirah resort next to Burj Al Arab, Al Qasr boasts a palatial gated entrance, opulent interiors and shares 1km (½ mile) of beach with the resort's other hotel, Mina A'Salam. Its restaurants include the excellent Pierchic, at the end of a wooden pier jutting into the Gulf from the hotel's gardens. For extra privacy, 29 summer houses, located around a picturesque network of canals, are also available.

Atlantis The Palm $$$$ *Palm Jumeira, tel: 04 426 0000, fax: 04 426 0001, email: info@atlantisthepalm.com, www.atlantisthe palm.com.* Having opened in style with a launch party that saw Hollywood's A-listers walk down the red carpet, this popular theme resort houses 1,373 lavish guest rooms and 166 suites – including the Lost Chambers with their mesmerising underwater views. With a dazzling mix of leisure facilities, retail outlets and eateries like Nobu and Ossiano, Atlantis The Palm is already an iconic tourist attraction.

Burj Al Arab $$$$$ *Jumeira Road, Umm Suqeim, tel: 04 301 7777, fax: 04 301 7000, email: baareservations@jumeirah.com, www. jumeirah.com.* A 'seven-star' all-suite hotel located on its own man-made island, the futuristic 'Tower of the Arabs' is claimed by its owners to be 'the world's most luxurious hotel' and in 2008 was voted the world's best hotel in the annual World Travel Awards. Known locally as 'the Burj', it's Dubai's most expensive hotel, not to mention its most famous landmark. Prices for a single night in one of its 202 two-storey suites, each with butler service, start at around $1,000. Access to the man-made island is restricted to hotel guests or non-guests with restaurant reservations.

Dubai Marine Beach Resort & Spa $$$ *Jumeira Road, Jumeira 1, tel: 04 346 1111, fax: 04 346 0234, email: dxbmarin@emirates. net.ae, www.dxbmarine.com.* Not to be confused with Dubai Marina along the coast, Dubai Marine is the closest Jumeira beach resort to the city, a short walk across Jumeira Road from Jumeira Mosque. It offers 195 rooms in villa-style low-rise buildings in a landscaped compound fronting on to a small beach. It also has some of the city's best nightspots, including Sho Cho and Boudoir.

Grosvenor House $$$ *Dubai Marina, tel: 04 399 8888, fax: 04 399 8444, email: reservations@lrm-gh-dubai.com, www.grosvenor house-dubai.com.* Although it's not located on the beach, this 45-

storey Le Meridien property offers stunning views of the coast, including The Palm Jumeirah and Dubai Marina. Guests can use the beach facilities at the nearby Le Royal Meridien Beach Resort. Notable nightspots at the hotel include Bar 44 and Buddha Bar.

Jumeirah Beach Hotel $$$$ *Jumeira Road, Umm Suqeim, tel: 04 348 0000, fax: 04 301 6800, email: jbhinfo@jumeirah.com, www. jumeirah.com.* Shaped like a breaking wave, to complement nearby Burj Al Arab's 'sail', the 26-storey Jumeirah Beach Hotel has 618 sea-facing rooms, 19 villas and 17 restaurants. This modern, international hotel lacks the Arabian atmosphere of Al Qasr, Mina A'Salam and One&Only Royal Mirage, but this didn't stop it being voted Best Resort in the World by the UK's *Business Traveller* magazine.

La Maison d'Hôtes $$ *Street 83B, Villa 18, Jumeirah, tel: 04 344 1838, fax: 344 6707, email: info@lamaisondhotesdubai.com, www. lamaisondhotesdubai.com.* If you're willing to overlook the fact that Dubai's only quaint boutique hotel does not serve alcohol, it's a gem of a place, providing an experience completely different to Dubai's other swanky hotels. Run by two French women, the hotel has 19 rooms, each of which is decorated in a different theme inspired by Oman, Persia, South Asia, bedouin and Berber cultures. All modern amenities are provided, including internet access, room service, two swimming pools and a fantastic French restaurant. Located within walking distance of the beach.

Mina A'Salam $$$$ *Al Sufouh Road, Umm Suqeim, tel: 04 366 8888, fax: 04 366 7788, email: mjinfo@jumeirah.com, www. jumeirah.com.* A shade less expensive than the nearby Al Qasr, the Madinat Jumeirah resort's second grand boutique hotel impresses with its fabulous reinvention of Arabian architecture and waterfront setting. Meaning 'Port of Peace', Mina A'Salam is connected via canals and walkways to Souk Madinat Jumeirah, with all its cafés, restaurants and bars, and via a slightly longer path to Wild Wadi Water Park and the Jumeirah Beach Hotel.

One&Only Royal Mirage $$$ *Al Sufouh Road, Al Sufouh, tel: 04 399 9999, fax: 04 399 9998, email: info@oneandonlyroyalmirage.ae,* *www.oneandonlyresorts.com*. Until Madinat Jumeirah opened in 2004, the Royal Mirage was the only hotel on the coast that could offer an Arabian (actually Moroccan) look and feel, and despite the competition it still takes some beating. Located on 1km (½ mile) of waterfront, the Royal Mirage offers 250 rooms in the Palace, 170 in the Arabian Court and 50 in the exclusive Residence & Spa. The hotel's venues include the restaurants Celebrities and Tagine and the Kasbar nightclub. It also has the Middle East's first Givenchy Spa. The Royal Mirage makes an appearance in the George Clooney–Matt Damon movie *Syriana*.

The Ritz-Carlton Dubai $$$ *Al Sufouh Road/Dubai Marina, tel: 04 399 4000, fax: 04 399 4001, email: reservation.dubai@ritz carlton.com, www.ritzcarlton.com.* A little bit of Andalusia in the Gulf, the low-lying *hacienda*-style Ritz-Carlton has 138 rooms, all sea-facing. More than any other hotel on the coast, it's a quiet retreat for rest and relaxation, far removed from the distractions and crowds of larger beach resorts. Its restaurants include the highly rated La Baie (French) and Splendido (Italian).

SHEIKH ZAYED ROAD

Crowne Plaza Dubai $$$ *Sheikh Zayed Road, tel: 04 331 1111, fax: 04 331 5555, email: crowneplaza@cpdubai.ae, www.dubaihotels. crowneplaza.com.* Located on the Satwa/Jumeira side of Sheikh Zayed Road, the venerable 568-room Crowne Plaza is convenient for delegates attending events at Dubai International Exhibition Centre, across the highway. Its restaurants include Trader Vic's and Wagamama. The popular nightclub Zinc is also in the hotel.

Fairmont Dubai $$$ *Sheikh Zayed Road, tel: 04 332 5555, fax: 04 332 4555, email: dubai@fairmont.com, www.fairmont.com.* The 394-room Fairmont stands on the Satwa/Jumeira side of Sheikh Zayed Road near the Trade Centre interchange. Notable for the glass pyramids on the four corners of its roof and its space-age atrium, the hotel is home to the excellent Spectrum On One restaurant and was the original home of one of Dubai's hippest club nights, Peppermint Lounge.

Ibis World Trade Centre $$ *Sheikh Zayed Road/Trade Centre 2, tel: 04 332 4444, fax: 04 331 1220, email: reservations@accorwtc. ae, www.ibishotel.com.* Compared to the generally high rack rates of Dubai hotels, the stylish, comfortable, four-star Ibis is one of the city's best-value offerings, but as the word spreads, the competition for its 210 rooms increases and it may be necessary to book several months in advance. Like its more expensive sister hotel, the Novotel, the French-owned Ibis adjoins the halls at Dubai International Exhibition Centre, making it a popular choice among business travellers during the October–May conference season.

Jumeirah Emirates Towers Hotel $$$ *Sheikh Zayed Road, tel: 04 330 0000, fax: 04 330 3030, email: jetinfo@jumeirah.com, www.jumeirah.com.* Part of the Jumeirah Group's portfolio, the landmark 305m (1,000ft) Emirates Towers Hotel has frequently been voted one of the world's best business hotels. Each of the 400 rooms over 51 floors has a dedicated workstation with ultra high-speed internet connection, wireless keyboard and fax/printer with private number. Its bars and restaurants include Vu's, the separate Vu's Bar, and The Agency.

The Palace – The Old Town $$$ *Burj Dubai Boulevard, Old Town, Downtown Burj Dubai, tel: 04 428 7888, fax: 04 428 7999, email: reservations@thepalace-dubai.com, www.theaddress.com.* The Palace – The Old Town is exactly what the name suggests – an opulent hotel reminiscent of an old Arabian palace. Only in this case, the traditional Arabesque facade is complemented with contemporary interiors that are no less luxurious than you would expect in a royal palace. It has views of a large artificial lake and the marvellous Burj Dubai, and is close to Dubai Mall, as well as to the business districts. There are three restaurants, including the excellent Thai Thiptara *(see page 140)*. 242 rooms.

Shangri-La Hotel $$$$ *Sheikh Zayed Road, tel: 04 343 8888, fax: 04 343 8886, email: sldb@shangri-la.com, www.shangri-la.com.* More expensive than the award-winning Emirates Towers – put it down to the sea views, which are better on the Satwa/Jumeira side of the highway – the 43-storey Shangri-La is located opposite the

Dusit Dubai near Interchange No. 1. It has 301 guest rooms and suites and 126 serviced apartments. Among its famous former guests is Hollywood star George Clooney, who filmed part of the movie *Syriana* in Dubai in 2004.

BUR DUBAI

Four Points Sheraton Bur Dubai $$$ *Khalid Bin Al Waleed Street (Bank Street), tel: 04 397 7444, fax: 04 397 7333, email: reservations. fps@starwoodhotels.com, www.fourpoints.com/burdubai.* Located in the heart of downtown Bur Dubai, the four-star, 125-room Four Points Sheraton is convenient for the creek and heritage sights such as Bastakiya, Al Fahidi Fort (Dubai Museum) and Bur Dubai Souk.

Golden Sands $$ *Between Mankhool Road and Sheikh Khalifa Bin Zayed Road (Trade Centre Road), tel: 04 355 5553, fax: 04 352 6903, email: reservation@goldensands.ae, www.goldensandsdubai. com.* Comprising 11 separate de-luxe apartment buildings rather than a star-rated hotel, Golden Sands offers self-catering options in the heart of the city that are popular with large families or groups that visit Dubai for events such as the Shopping Festival and Rugby Sevens. The more people sharing, the cheaper the cost, though for singles, couples and small families, the facilities don't justify the four-star pricing.

Grand Hyatt Dubai $$$ *Sheikh Rashid Road, Umm Hurair 2, tel: 04 317 1234, fax: 04 317 1235, email: dubai.grand@hyatt.com, www.dubai.grand.hyatt.com.* A rare resort-type hotel in the centre of the city, the 674-room Grand Hyatt lies roughly half-way between the airport and Sheikh Zayed Road. The central location makes the hotel a good base for sightseeing or business meetings on either side of the creek, though nearby Garhoud Bridge is a traffic bottleneck during the morning and evening rush hour. The hotel is also convenient for Wafi and zipping along Route 44 towards Nad Al Sheba, Al Ain or the Hatta road.

Jumeira Rotana Hotel $$$ *Al Dhiyafah Road, Satwa, tel: 04 345 5888, fax: 04 345 8777, email: jumeira.hotel@rotana.com, www.*

rotana.com. The 'Satwa Rotana', a much less catchy name, would be a more accurate description of this four-star, 114-room hotel's location on Al Dhiyafah Street in Satwa, but it's nevertheless a good base for forays along the coast on nearby Jumeira Road. The heritage attractions of Shindagha and Bur Dubai lie at the other end of nearby Mina ('Port') Road, and Sheikh Zayed Road is a short cab ride in another direction. Its popular Boston Bar is based on the watering-hole in the American TV series *Cheers*.

Seashell Inn Hotel $$ *Khalid Bin Al Waleed Street (Bank Street), tel: 04 393 4777, fax: 04 393 4466, email: shellinn@emirates.net.ae, www.landmarkhotelsdubai.com.* This three-star, 105-room city centre hotel in the heart of downtown Bur Dubai is within walking distance of the heritage areas of Shindagha, Bur Dubai Souk, Al Fahidi Fort (Dubai Museum) and Bastakiya.

XVA Gallery Hotel $$ *Bastakiya, tel: 04 353 5383, fax: 04 353 5988, email: xva@xvagallery.com, www.xvagallery.com.* No other paid accommodation in Dubai can compete with the XVA Gallery's authentic Arabian offering. More a guesthouse than a hotel – too small to qualify for a star-rating – the XVA is first and foremost an art gallery and coffee shop set around the inner courtyard of a restored home in the city's historic Bastakiya district. Its eight guest rooms, furnished in the Arabian-style, are on the first-floor rooftop, which offers wonderful views of the creek skyline, in particular the wind-towers on nearby buildings. A delightful, inspirational haven for artists and writers in particular.

DEIRA

Al Bustan Rotana $$ *Casablanca Street, Garhoud, tel: 04 282 0000, fax: 04 282 8100, email: albustan.hotel@rotana.com, www.rotana.com.* For a five-star hotel, the 275-room Al Bustan Rotana offers very good value for money. Located close to the airport, on the road to Garhoud Bridge, it has excellent health and fitness facilities, including a gymnasium, tennis and squash courts, and a swimming pool. Its restaurants, including the Japanese Benihana and Thai Blue Elephant, are among the best in town.

Hilton Dubai Creek $$$ *Baniyas Road, tel: 04 227 1111, fax: 04 227 1131, email: info_dubai-creek@hilton.com, www.hilton.co.uk/ dubaicreek*. Designed by Carlos Ott, the 154-room Hilton Dubai Creek is a stylish contemporary hotel set back from the creek on the land side of Baniyas Road. Nevertheless, its creek-facing rooms offer outstanding views of the nearby *dhow* wharves, as well as the distant Sheikh Zayed Road skyline. The hotel's French restaurant Verre is British celebrity chef Gordon Ramsay's first restaurant outside the UK and one of the city's best.

Hyatt Regency Dubai $$$ *Corniche Road, tel: 04 209 1234, fax: 04 209 1235, email: dubai.regency@hyatt.com, www.dubai.regency. hyatt.com*. A recent refurbishment has given a new lease of life to the venerable 414-room Hyatt Regency, a distinctive dark monolith overlooking the mouth of Dubai Creek. All rooms have sea views, the higher floors offering a unique perspective on The Palm Deira. Its popular restaurants include the Mediterranean Focaccia and the Japanese Miyako. The hotel also has Dubai's only revolving restaurant, the roof-top Al Dawaar.

Park Hyatt $$$ *Dubai Creek Golf & Yacht Club, tel: 04 602 1234, fax: 04 602 1235, email: dubai.park@hyatt.com, www.dubai.park. hyatt.com*. One of 27 Park Hyatt hotels around the world when it opened in 2005 and the first in the Middle East, this hotel is positioned as a 'city-centre luxury retreat', which is a credible claim given its private creekside setting next to Dubai Creek Golf and Yacht Club. Deira City Centre and the Aviation Club tennis and restaurant complex are nearby.

Radisson SAS $$$ *Baniyas Road, tel: 04 222 7171, fax: 04 228 4777, email: reservations.deira.dubai@radissonblu.com, www.deira creek.dubai.radissonsas.com*. The first chain hotel in Dubai when it opened as the InterCon in 1975, the 276-room Radisson SAS remains a firm favourite thanks to its central location overlooking the creek. Among the hotel's venues are the hip Italian restaurant La Moda and Up On The 10th, one of the best live jazz venues in town. The *dhow* wharves are within walking distance and the Deira souks are a short cab ride away.

UAE Youth Hostel Association $ *Al Nahda Road, Al Ghusais, tel: 04 298 8151, fax: 04 298 8141, email: uaeyha@emirates.net.ae, www.uaeyha.com.* At Dhs220 (US$60) per room, by international standards Dubai youth hostel is expensive, but relative to the Dubai market, the rooms here are an absolute bargain. Located on the Al Mulla Plaza side of Dubai International Airport, the standards in this well-managed hostel can be likened to some three-star hotels.

OUTSIDE THE CITY

Al Maha Desert Resort & Spa $$$$$ *Interchange No. 8, Dubai-Al Ain Road, tel: 04 303 4222, fax: 04 343 9696, email: almaha@emirates.com, www.al-maha.com.* The Al Maha eco-resort, 40km (25 miles) from Dubai, is a world-class destination with prices to match. Resembling a luxury tented camp within the 225sq km (87sq mile) Dubai Desert Conservation Reserve, the 'six-star' resort is named after the Arabian oryx *(al maha)* that live and breed in the surrounding dunes. Each of its 40 suites has a private pool. Horse riding, camel trekking and falconry are among the activities for guests, in addition to the spa and leisure centre, library and Gallery retail outlet.

Hatta Fort Hotel $$ *Hatta, tel: 04 852 3211, fax: 04 852 3561, email: hfh@jaihotels.com, www.jebelali-international.com.* Before the Al Maha resort and Bab Al Shams, the four-star Hatta Fort Hotel was the only retreat from the city that promised a bit of luxury pampering and adventure. Set among the mountains of the Hajar range, near the border with Oman, an hour's drive from Dubai, the Hatta Fort may be a little dated now, but its appeal is enduring. Its 50 chalets have views of the mountains, which can be explored on 4x4 trips arranged by the hotel.

Jumeirah Bab Al Shams Desert Resort & Spa $$$ *Endurance City, tel: 04 809 6100, fax: 04 832 6698, email: jbasinfo@jumeirah.com, www.jumeirah.com.* If the budget won't stretch to Al Maha, consider Bab Al Shams (literally 'Gate of the Sun') in a desert-fort setting among the dunes near Dubai's centre for endurance riding, 37km (23 miles) from Dubai Autodrome.

Recommended Restaurants

With so many world-class hotels, it's not surprising that Dubai also has many world-class restaurants. But several of the city's most interesting and popular eateries aren't in hotels. Beloved by locals and expats of all nationalities, these venues can be off the tourist trail and hard to find, but they're worth seeking out if you want to combine great food and atmosphere with a glimpse of daily life in this cosmopolitan melting pot. Just remember that non-hotel venues aren't licensed to serve alcohol: if you absolutely must have wine with your meal, your options are restricted to hotels and clubs. If you opt for a hotel restaurant, it is advisable to make a reservation in advance.

Many restaurants near tourist sights are mentioned in passing in the *Where to Go* and *Eating Out* sections, but are not necessarily included in this list, which amounts to a 'best of'. Once you have worked your way through the list and perhaps revisited your favourites, get hold of one of the inexpensive, locally published eating out guides from *Time Out Dubai*, *What's On* or Explorer Publishing for more suggestions.

The price categories below are based on the average cost of a meal for two with a glass of wine each in hotel venues, or soft drinks elsewhere. *Bil-hana!* Bon appétit!

$$$$$	More than Dhs500
$$$$	Dhs400–500
$$$	Dhs200–400
$$	Dhs100–200
$	Less than Dhs100

DUBAI

JUMEIRA COAST

Al Mahara $$$$$ *Burj Al Arab, Jumeira Road, tel: 04 301 7600.* The seafood venue at Burj Al Arab is reportedly Dubai's most expensive restaurant and certainly one of the city's plushest. Its centrepiece is the mother of all fish tanks – almost an aquarium in size. The dress code is semi-formal, and men are expected to wear a jacket at dinner; no jeans. Open daily 12.30–3pm and 7pm–11.30pm.

Japengo $$–$$$ *Palm Strip Shopping Mall, Jumeira Road, tel: 04 345 4979.* The original outlet in a Dubai franchise from the always reliable Bin Hendi group (its other brands include La Brioche and Café Havana), Japengo is a fashionable street café that has an interesting international menu with a strong Asian influence. Open Fri–Wed 10am–1am, Thur 10am–2am.

Lime Tree Café $–$$ *Jumeira Road, tel: 04 349 8498.* Run by New Zealanders, the understatedly hip Lime Tree occupies two floors of a stylishly converted villa with outdoor seating. Reminiscent of an arts-centre café, its wholesome specialities – all the food is homemade – include the best carrot cake in Dubai. Open daily 7.30am–6pm.

Pierchic $$$$$ *Al Qasr, Madinat Jumeirah, tel: 04 366 6730.* A fabulous seafood venue at the end of a wooden pier with stunning views of the Madinat Jumeirah resort and Burj Al Arab. Open daily noon–3pm and 7–11.30pm

Tagine $$$ *One&Only Royal Mirage, Al Sufouh Road, tel: 04 399 9999.* An atmospheric Moroccan restaurant in an attractive resort hotel. Open Tue–Sun 7–11.30pm.

Zheng He's $$$$ *Mina A'Salam, Madinat Jumeirah, tel: 04 366 6730.* A wonderful Chinese restaurant with outdoor seating overlooking a canal in one of the Madinat Jumeirah resort's stunning hotels. Excellent *dim sum*. Open daily noon–3pm and 7–11.30pm.

SHEIKH ZAYED ROAD

Al Nafoorah $$$ *Emirates Towers Boulevard, tel: 04 319 8088.* The best Lebanese restaurant in Dubai. Its dishes are pricey, but the business-lunch menu offers very good value for money. *Shisha* (waterpipe) available. Open daily 12.30–4pm and 8pm–midnight.

The Noodle House $$$ *Emirates Towers Boulevard, tel: 04 319 8758.* Popular Asian fusion restaurant with bench and table seating that's crowded with office workers at lunchtimes. Open daily noon–midnight.

Spectrum On One $$$$$ *The Fairmont Dubai, tel: 04 311 8101.* A stylish restaurant in a hip hotel serving good food from eight separate open kitchens – Szechuan, Thai, Japanese, Indian, European, etc. Open daily 6.30pm–1am.

Teatro $$$ *Towers Rotana, tel: 04 343 8000.* Serving up five different cuisines, this lively restaurant has a theatrical theme but happily lacks drama and pretension. Open daily 6pm–2am.

Thiptara $$$$$ *The Palace – The Old Town, Downtown Burj Dubai, tel: 04 428 7961.* Few restaurants in Dubai have such a stunning combination of decor and cuisine as Thiptara, the Thai restaurant at The Palace – The Old Town hotel. While the prices are high, it's highly unlikely that you would walk out with even the slightest hint of disappointment. Open daily 7pm–midnight.

Vu's $$$$$ *Jumeirah Emirates Towers Hotel, tel: 04 319 8088.* One of the highest restaurants in the Middle East, on the 50th floor of a landmark hotel, the French Vu's offers stunning views and modern European cooking of the highest quality – and prices. Open daily 12.30–3pm and 7.30pm–midnight.

BUR DUBAI

Al Dahleez $$ *Al Boom Tourist Village, Umm Hurair, tel: 04 324 3000.* A creekside Arabic buffet restaurant offering regional dishes, including hard-to-find Emirati food. Popular with local families – a sure sign of authenticity. Open daily noon–4pm and 7pm–midnight.

Bastakiah Nights $$$ *Bastakiya, tel: 04 353 7772.* Good Arabic and Iranian food served in a fine-dining environment in the wonderful setting of a historic house in the creekside Bastakiya district. Open daily 12.30–11.30pm.

Bateaux Dubai $$$$$ *Al Seef Road, tel: 04 399 4994*. This floating restaurant offers an international à la carte menu as well as a constantly changing view of the creek skyline. Boarding for the dinner cruise is on Al Seef Road at 7.45pm daily.

Chhappan Bhog $ *Sheikh Khalifa Bin Zayed Road (Trade Centre Road), Karama, tel: 04 396 8176*. A friendly, street-level Indian restaurant that specialises in vegetarian *thali*, the various small metal containers of which are regularly refilled. Open daily 12.30–2.30pm and 8–11.30pm.

Kan Zaman $ *Shindagha creekside, tel: 04 393 9913*. Meaning 'Once upon a time', this Arabic restaurant with outdoor seating has a delightful creekside setting, but because of its proximity to heritage sites it can be swamped by large organised tour groups. *Shisha* pipes available.

Ravi's $ *Near Satwa Roundabout, tel: 04 331 5353*. Thanks to its superb curries (with meat), this street-level Pakistani restaurant has become a Dubai institution. Two people can eat very well for less than Dhs50. Open Sat–Thur 5am–3am, Fri 5am–noon and 1.30pm–3am.

DEIRA

Al Mansour $$$$ *Radisson SAS, tel: 04 222 7171*. A dinner cruise with an Arabic and international buffet on a traditional *dhow* that plies the creek. Boarding from the Deira creekside near the Radisson SAS at 8pm daily.

Blue Elephant $$$ *Al Bustan Rotana Hotel, Garhoud, tel: 04 282 0000*. One of Dubai's best Thai restaurants, Blue Elephant has an interior 'garden' setting just off the hotel's main lobby. Open noon–3pm and 7pm–midnight.

The Boardwalk $$ *Dubai Creek Golf and Yacht Club, tel: 04 295 6000*. The combination of good food and delightful open-air setting above the creek near the marina at Dubai Creek Golf and Yacht Club has helped make The Boardwalk a Dubai institution.

Noted for its seafood, including fish and chips. Open daily 8am–midnight.

Focaccia $$$ *Hyatt Regency, Corniche Road, Deira, tel: 04 317 2222.* Still going strong after more than a decade, Focaccia offers Italian cuisine in an indoor recreation of a Mediterranean villa. Don't miss the delicious roasted garlic that's served with the eponymous bread. Open daily 12.30–3pm and 7pm–midnight.

Kiku $$$ *Le Meridien Dubai, Airport Road, tel: 04 282 4040.* Kiku's enduring popularity among visiting Japanese businessmen confirms its reputation as one of the best Japanese restaurants in the city. Open daily 12.30–2.45pm and 6.30–11pm.

Mazaj $$$ *Century Village, The Aviation Club, Garhoud, tel: 04 282 9952.* A popular Lebanese restaurant that fronts onto the plaza at Century Village in the Aviation Club. Opt for the set menu: the food just keeps on coming. The club setting means that alcohol is served. *Shisha* pipes available. Open daily 11am–1am.

More $$ *Behind Lifco Supermarket, near Welcare Hospital, Garhoud, tel: 04 283 0224.* A funky Dutch-owned bistro that is popular with media types who work nearby and Emirates cabin crew who live in the surrounding buildings. The international menu offers amazing choice. More can't be beaten for atmosphere, quality, value and service. Open daily 8am–11pm.

Reflets Par Pierre Gagnaire $$$$$ *InterContinental Dubai, Festival City, tel: 04 701 1111.* The newest addition to Dubai's culinary scene combines sumptuous interiors with Gagnaire's four-course meals and exquisite champagne. Open daily 7–11pm.

Verre $$$$$ *Hilton Dubai Creek, Baniyas Road, tel: 04 212 7551.* As you might expect from British celebrity chef Gordon Ramsay's first restaurant outside the UK, Verre offers exceptional quality French cuisine in surroundings of understated elegance. A truly world-class restaurant that has helped put Dubai on the culinary map. Open Sun–Fri 7pm–midnight.

INDEX

Berlitz pocket guide

Dubai

Second Edition 2008
Updated 2009

Written by Matt Jones
Updated by Shweta Parida
Series Editor: Tony Halliday

Photography credits
All images by Matt Jones except: 8, 82 Getty
Images; 57, 73 iStockphoto; 20 Topham.

Cover picture: Balkis Press/ABACA/
PA Photos

Printed in Singapore by Insight Print
Services (Pte) Ltd, 38 Joo Koon Road,
Singapore 628990. Tel: (65) 6865-1600.
Fax: (65) 6861-6438

Berlitz Trademark Reg. U.S. Patent Office
and other countries. Marca Registrada

Every effort has been made to provide
accurate information in this publication,
but changes are inevitable. The publisher
cannot be responsible for any resulting
loss, inconvenience or injury.

Contact us

At Berlitz we strive to keep our guides as
accurate and up to date as possible, but if you
find anything that has changed, or if you have
any suggestions on ways to improve this guide,
then we would be delighted to hear from you.

Berlitz Publishing, PO Box 7910,
London SE1 1WE, England.
fax (44) 20 7403 0290
email: berlitz@apaguide.co.uk
www.berlitzpublishing.com